Bucks Point Lacemaking

Pamela Nottingham

B.T. Batsford Ltd, London

Also by Pamela Nottingham and published by Batsford:
The Technique of Bobbin Lace
The Technique of Torchon Lace
The Technique of Bucks Point Lace
Bobbin Lace Making
Bedfordshire Lace Making

I appreciate very much the help and encouragement that I receive from my husband, Arthur Johnson and again thank him for his patience and skill in producing all the illustrations. Through the craft of bobbin lace making I have made many friends, in Britain and overseas, and I should like to thank them for their interest and enthusiasm.

© Pamela Nottingham 1985
First published 1985
Reprinted in paperback 1992

ISBN 0 7134 2235 1

Filmset by Servis Filmsetting Ltd, Manchester

Printed and bound in Great Britain by
The Bath Press
Avon
for the publishers B.T. Batsford Ltd
4 Fitzhardinge Street, London W1H 0AH

Contents

Preface

Today there is an ever-increasing interest in traditional English lace, particularly in Bucks Point, which is often considered to be the most intricate of all bobbin laces. In the past the craft was passed on from mother to daughter or learnt in the small cottage lace school. A few skilled workers made fans, collars and elaborate flounces but the majority of lacemakers produced lace edgings in black, white or ecru with matching gimp thread. I prefer to see the old laces worked in the traditional way and colour reserved for modern designs.

The first fourteen patterns here are traditional – made throughout the nineteenth century in the East Midland villages. Patterns were recognised by name, usually of wild flowers, birds or animals; only names known to be authentic are used in this book, I leave the lacemaker to speculate on those long forgotten.

The patterns in the first section are arranged as a progression. To make any lace successfully it is necessary to 'read' the pattern, recognise the features and develop a good basic knowledge of stitches and technique. Always remember that it is very important to *understand* the reasons for working in a particular way. There are so many attractive patterns that the aim of every lacemaker must be to take a pricking and make the lace, perhaps a pricking that has not been worked for a hundred years, and to re-introduce it to the lacemaking world. This is the challenge and enjoyment that awaits the enthusiast. The diagrams that accompany photographs and prickings are to assist the learning process and are not an essential requirement for every new pattern.

Hexagons, samplers and six section roundels are not found among the old patterns; these are a modern adaptation to give the twentieth-century lacemaker opportunity to complete lace quickly and put it to some imaginative use. Of the twenty-seven patterns in the last section, twenty-four have been designed for a variety of mounts – frames, brooches, boxes, etc., and the last three, two jabots and cuffs, to enhance the appearance and give pleasure to the wearer. Appendix A contains a collection of prickings from the first section, either enlarged or reduced. Fine patterns are suitable for baby clothes and enlarged patterns are given to help anyone experiencing difficulty. Always ascertain that the lace is the correct size for the mount, if necessary the pricking can be adjusted using a modern photocopier.

Most people have an understanding of bobbin lace methods before beginning Bucks Point lace, but this is not essential and it is possible to begin lacemaking using this book. Refer to Appendix B for additional information.

The quality of the finished lace depends on the accuracy of the pricking and the use of card in which holes do not become enlarged and distorted by pins. Bucks Point lace is rarely made with the holes on the footside more than 2mm apart; a fine two cord thread and soft gimp are essential. The use of thick thread and a pricking with holes far apart may facilitate the working but the result cannot be called Bucks Point lace! The beauty is lost and the enthusiasm of the lacemaker gone for ever. In the last section, some photographs show the lace natural size, these show the neat hexagonal net ground and the closeness of passive pairs with picots. I have deliberately used a fine thread in the first section so that the lacemaker can trace the movement of threads. For the same reason the photographs show the lace much enlarged; it is distressing to see lace appear unattractive and imperfections magnified but hopefully it will assist the lacemaker.

In the text I have made no mention of pillows and bobbins, I recommend the lacemaker to start with equipment with which she is familiar – the exception being the small Honiton pillow and lightweight bobbins. Traditionally the spangled East Midland bobbins or short thick South Bucks bobbins were used on square or bolster pillows, the slim spangled bobbins are preferred by many lacemakers as they take up little room and do not roll on the pillow.

I hope this small book will provide the lacemaker with the basic knowledge of Bucks Point lace to enable her to make and enjoy the most beautiful of our English laces.

Preparation
one

Thread

Patterns with holes 2.5mm ($\frac{1}{10}$ inch) apart on the footside or vertical rows of ground: D.M.C. Retors D'Alsace no. 30; 120/2 linen thread
Patterns with holes 2mm ($\frac{1}{12}$ inch) apart on the footside or vertical rows of ground: D.M.C. Retors D'Alsace no. 50
Throughout this book D.M.C. Pearl cotton no. 8 is used as a gimp thread. This outlines and accentuates the pattern features.
Bobbins are always wound in pairs, refer to Appendix B.

Pins

Fine brass or stainless steel pins with small heads, approximately 25mm (1 inch), are recommended.

Pricking board and pricker

A flat piece of cork or polystyrene and four drawing pins.
A slim pinvice or pricker with a Sharp no. 8 sewing needle. It is necessary to keep the pricker in a vertical position when working. A thick or bulbous pricker is usually held at an angle in order to see the holes, the pricking will be irregular and the lace distorted.

To prepare the pricking

Preparation of Bucks Point prickings is a tedious task as the holes are very close together, the following procedure should be used:

(i) Make a photocopy of the pricking. One is allowed to take one copy for personal use without infringing copyright.
(ii) On the pricking board place a piece of pricking card slightly larger than the pattern. Over this place a piece of white paper the same size as the card.
Put the photocopy on top and fasten securely together using four drawing pins, one at each corner.
(iii) If the pattern has a footside or picot holes in a straight line, prick and place a pin in one hole at either end. Push a straight edge against the pins and prick the line of holes, this will ensure accuracy.
(iv) Refer to diagram 1. Prick in the diagonal rows of holes, if necessary mark the vertical rows with a hard pencil to achieve a regular grid.
(v) Prick the curves and picots.
(vi) Remove the photocopy and indicate the gimp lines on card and paper copies in pencil. When correct, mark in permanent black ink.

Additional information for pricking complicated patterns

(i) Arrange card, paper and photocopy as described above.
(ii) Prick in the pattern features and the picots.
(iii) Carefully separate the copies to mark in the gimp lines.
(iv) Reassemble and check the position is correct by using the point of the pricker. The large posts on drawing pins facilitate this reassembly.
(v) Complete the pricking.
   It cannot be overemphasised that honeycomb

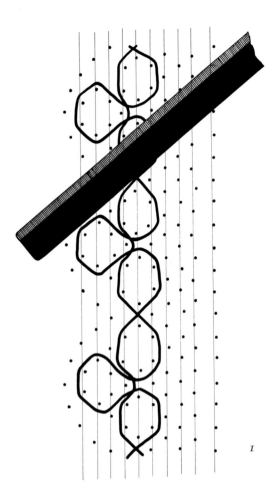

I

and ground should be geometrically accurate but
that flowers, leaves and other features may rely on
curves to give a pleasing design, *never* place them
on grid lines to the detriment of the pattern.
Obviously there will be added difficulties when
making the lace, but after the basic techniques have
been mastered, this is the true challenge of Bucks
Point lace.

two Basic Stitches

All stitches depend on the use of four threads – two pairs – making some combination of two movements, cross (a) and twist (b). Refer to diagram 2.

Cloth stitch   aba

Half stitch   ab   this is rarely used in Bucks Point lace

Ground stitch   abbb   this stitch is NEVER covered

Honeycomb stitch   abb   this stitch is always covered. abb PIN abb

Twisting of threads   threads of a pair are sometimes twisted, right over left, once or several times to improve appearance and increase the strength. For example:

(i) As the weaver passes round the pin, two twists are given to the weaver pair.

(ii) Cloth stitch and three twists is a stitch that is always used at the footside edge. It is worked aba bbb and *BOTH* pairs are twisted.

Stitch practice

To revise cloth stitch and learn the footside edge sequence the practice strip in photograph 3 is made.

Prepare six pairs of bobbins and pricking 4. Refer to diagram 5.

Place six pins in the six holes at the top, and hang one pair round each pin.

Use the right-hand pair on pin G as weaver and work a cloth stitch with the adjacent pair. Discard that pair to the right of the pillow.

Work cloth stitch with the weaver and the next pair, discard this pair to the right of the pillow.

Continue with cloth stitch through the three

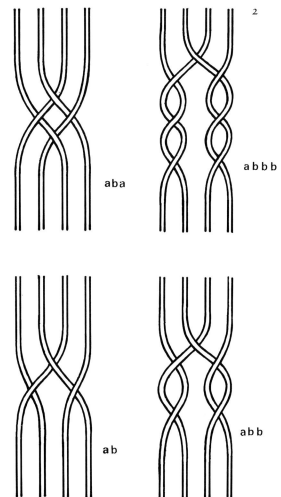

2

aba

a b b b

a b

a b b

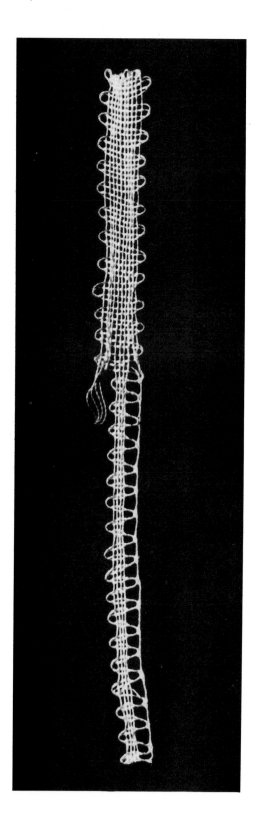

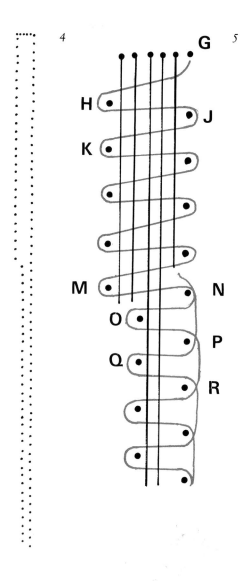

remaining pairs, the weaver pair is on the left-hand side. Twist the weaver twice and put up pin H to the right of the weaver pair.

Use the weaver and the pair to the right of it to make a cloth stitch, discard one pair to the left of the pillow.

Work a cloth stitch with the weaver and the next pair, discard the pair to the left of the pillow.

Continue with cloth stitch through the three remaining pairs, the weaver is on the right-hand side. Twist the weaver pair twice and put up pin J to the left of the weaver pair.

Continue to pin M.

Work to the right through four pairs in cloth stitch. Twist the weaver and the remaining pair three times each, and then work cloth stitch and three twists (three twists on both pairs). Put up pin N to the left of both pairs. Discard the outside pair to the right of the pillow. Take the left-hand pair and weave through two pairs in cloth stitch. Twist the weaver three times, and put up pin O.

The remaining two pairs are no longer required and should be cut off.

Footside sequence

Take the fourth pair from the right and work cloth stitch to the right through two passive pairs.
Twist the weaver three times.
Work cloth stitch and three twists on the outside edge.
Put up pin P to the left of both pairs.
Ignore the outer pair.
Work the inner pair back through the two passive pairs in cloth stitch.
Twist the weaver three times.
(In order to practise this edge a pin must support the weaver on this side, put up pin Q to the right of the weaver pair.)
The sequence must be memorised and fully understood before attempting the edgings in the next section.
Note: the weaver pairs alternate on the straight edge (known as the footside edge), there are no stitches round the pins. One stitch only is worked at the edge. The passive pairs are worked in cloth stitch and are never twisted.

Technical Terms

Footside. The straight edge which is sewn onto the fabric, it is on the right-hand side when making lace. When working an insertion it occurs on both sides.
Headside (or Head). The decorative edge of the lace, it usually has picots.
Ground. In Bucks Point lace the hexagonal net.
Catch Pin. The first ground pin put in position adjacent to the two passive pairs. It is important that the pin goes to the side of both pairs after the stitch has been made, and that another stitch is made before the next pin is put in position.
Filling. The decorative effect achieved by various stitches to cover an area within the design, e.g. honeycomb.

Instruction details

After initial explanation has been given, instruction will be limited as follows:
Work ground pin x. Work a ground stitch and put up the pin between the pairs.
Work catch pin x. Work a ground stitch and put up the pin to the side of both pairs.
Work honeycomb pin x. Work the honeycomb stitch, put up the pin and cover with the second honeycomb stitch.
Pass pairs round the gimp. The appropriate twists to enclose the gimp thread must be given as necessary. Refer to page 13.
Pass the gimp thread through pairs. The instruction above applies.

three Lace Edgings

Traditionally Bucks Point lace has always been made by the yard. Many of the beautiful flounces made in the eighteenth century were 400mm (16 inches) wide and required many hundreds of bobbins. The fourteen edgings selected for inclusion in this book are nineteenth-century designs, but the author has added corners for the lacemaker who wishes to make handkerchiefs. In the past the lace was gathered around the corner, it looks most attractive but the method is little used today.

Inexperienced lacemakers are advised to work many lengths of lace until the principles are fully understood. Before working any corner, reference should be made to page 45 where the method is explained in detail. The patterns are arranged as a progression and it is recommended that they are worked in the order given. Each can be mounted to make a handkerchief, overall measurement approximately 225mm (9 inches). The size of the linen required for mounting will vary according to the width of the lace.

The pricking

For handkerchiefs two copies should be made. In order to check continuity the same horizontal row of holes has been pricked at both ends. All prickings must be cut as indicated by the lines aa on the fan pattern, pricking 7.

For a continuous strip, the holes ringed across the pricking indicate the position for matching the pattern.

In Appendix A several prickings are repeated, either larger for those people who initially may experience difficulty working with holes so close

together, or smaller for use with finer thread where a truly dainty lace is required.

Pattern 1. The Bucks Fan. Photograph 6.

Prepare thirteen pairs of bobbins, a single gimp bobbin and pricking 7. Refer to diagram 8.
To begin. Place pins in holes A to H.
Hang two pairs round pin A, two pairs side by side on pin B and one pair on each pin, C to H.
Twist threads either side of A three times and work cloth stitch and three twists to cover pin A.
Ignore the right-hand pair. Using the other pair work to the left with cloth stitch through the two pairs hanging on B. (These passive pairs remain straight throughout and are never twisted.)
Twist the weaver three times, and work a ground stitch with the pair from C.
Put up the catch pin 2 to the right of both pairs.
Ignore the right-hand pair. Use the left-hand pair and the pair from D to work a ground stitch and put up pin 3 between these pairs.
Ignore the right-hand pair. Use the left-hand pair and the pair from E to work a ground stitch and put up pin 4 between these pairs.
Ignore the right-hand pair. Use the left-hand pair and the pair from F to work a ground stitch and put up pin 5 between the pairs.
Similarly work ground pins 6 and 7.
Remove support pins C to H inclusive. Do not remove pin B yet.
Footside and ground: Take the fourth pair from the footside (right hand) edge.
Work cloth stitch to the right through two passive pairs.

Twist the weaver three times.

Work cloth stitch and three twists (on both pairs) with the edge pair.

Put up pin 8 to the left of both pairs.

Ignore the right-hand pair and use the other pair to work cloth stitch back through the two passive pairs.

Twist the weaver three times.

Catch pin: Work a ground stitch with this weaver and the next pair to the left.

Put up the catch pin 9 to the right of both pairs.

Ground: Ignore the right-hand pair and use the other and next to the left to work a ground stitch, put up pin 10 between the pairs.

Complete the diagonal row of ground, including pin 13.

Work the footside and ground diagonally from pin 14. Remember to work to the footside edge with the fourth pair from the edge. Work similarly from 19 to 22.

General information concerning footside and ground

For accuracy check that:
1. The edge is straight.
2. There are two cloth passive pairs.
3. No threads hang between the catch pin and the passive pairs.
4. Two pairs hang between the catch pin and the next diagonal ground pin.
5. Along the diagonal ground row, one pair hangs between the pins.
6. At the end of every diagonal row, the bobbin on the extreme left can be pulled taut and traced back to the footside pin. Failure to achieve this results from inaccurate twisting when ground stitches are made.
7. If the right-hand thread of any pair hanging in ground is pulled, the thread can be traced diagonally as it should have travelled from left to right.

Gimp thread

This is the soft thread which outlines the pattern features. Lace threads usually travel diagonally across the lace and the gimp thread is passed through as follows:

When the gimp is moving to the right, it is placed under the left thread and over the right thread.

When the gimp is moving to the left, it is placed over the right thread and under the left thread.

Regardless of direction the gimp thread always lies under the left thread and over the right thread.

A gimp thread is always enclosed by twists. If the pair comes from ground or honeycomb, it is ready twisted and no additional twists are required. After the gimp thread twists are needed in preparation for the next stitches, i.e. two before honeycomb and three before ground. Two twists are given before and after cloth stitch.

Refer to the instructions on page 15, diagram 8.

To work the fan: Hang a single gimp thread on a pin at H. Pass it through four pairs from the ground (pins 7 to 22) and twist each pair twice. Hang three pairs in order on a pin at J. Use the left-hand pair as weaver and work in cloth stitch through three pairs (two from J and one from pin 7). Put up pin k to the left of the weaver pair.

Twist the weaver twice and weave back to the outer (left-hand) edge. Put up pin m to the right of the weaver pair.

Twist the weaver twice, and weave back in cloth stitch through four pairs (three pairs already in the fan and one from pin 13). Put up pin n to the left of the weaver pair.

Twist the weaver twice and weave through the four pairs to the outside edge.

Continue to work in cloth stitch bringing in pairs at p and r. Working from the outside back to t note that cloth stitch is worked through five pairs only. One pair is left hanging after r, t and v. The weaver remains the same throughout. The weaver is left on the outside edge, uncovered as soon as pin x is in position.

Twist the pairs hanging from r, t, v and w twice each, pass the gimp thread over the first and under the second thread of each pair. Twist these pairs three times in preparation for the ground.

Remove pin B which supports the footside passives and ease the threads into place.

One pattern repeat is complete.

To achieve good tension, check the following:

1. All threads in footside and ground should be pulled firmly every time a stitch is made. The bobbins must be heavy enough to keep the threads taut and there should be a definite slope on the pillow to maintain this tension.
2. The passive threads in the fan require particular care. On the curved edge the pairs should be eased around the curve, never pulled as this will destroy

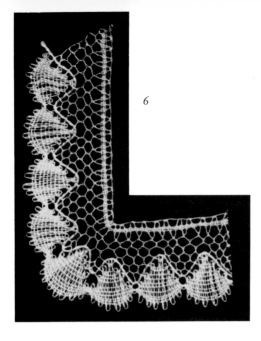

6

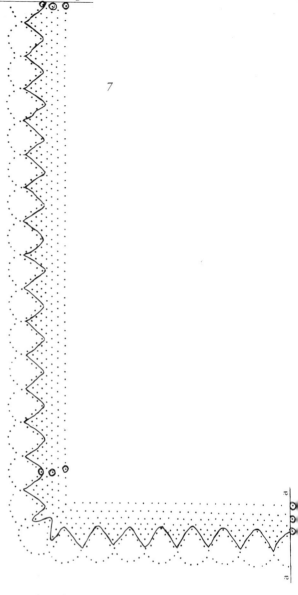

7

the fan shape. In the centre and on the right side the threads should be pulled firmly. Some lacemakers refer to 'stroking' the bobbins, i.e. moving the hands vertically down the bobbins at the end of a row of ground or when working cloth stitch. This is an excellent action as it helps to achieve good tension.

The corner

Work footside and ground from pins 1 to 6.
Work footside (corner) pin, catch pin and ground stitch from a to c.
Pass the gimp to the right through four pairs, the last being the pair from the left-hand side of pin c. Twist each pair twice.
Work corner fan from x to x. Note that pin f is worked after three cloth stitches and nothing has entered through the gimp from the ground.
Twist the pairs from the fan twice each, take the gimp from the point of the fan to the left through four pairs. Twist these pairs three times each. The last two pairs through the gimp work a ground stitch and pin g is placed between them. Refer to the diagram and work a ground stitch and pin h. The pair from the point of the fan and the pair to the right of it work a ground stitch and pin d. Pairs from h and d work a ground stitch and pin j. The gimp passes to the right through these pairs from g, h and j.
Work the fan, noting that three cloth stitches are worked before pin k, but nothing enters from the

ground at this pin.
To continue: Pairs from the right of d and the left of b work a ground stitch and catch pin e is placed to the right of both pairs. From pin e work the long row of ground (as from 3 to 7 in the original instruction).
Take the fourth pair from the edge and work out to the footside where the corner pin a is used a second time. To do this, remove the pin and allow the threads it enclosed to be pushed back so that the hole will be used for the second time with the second threads. It looks untidy when the threads are wound around and the pin supports both stitches. Continue with the catch pin and ground.

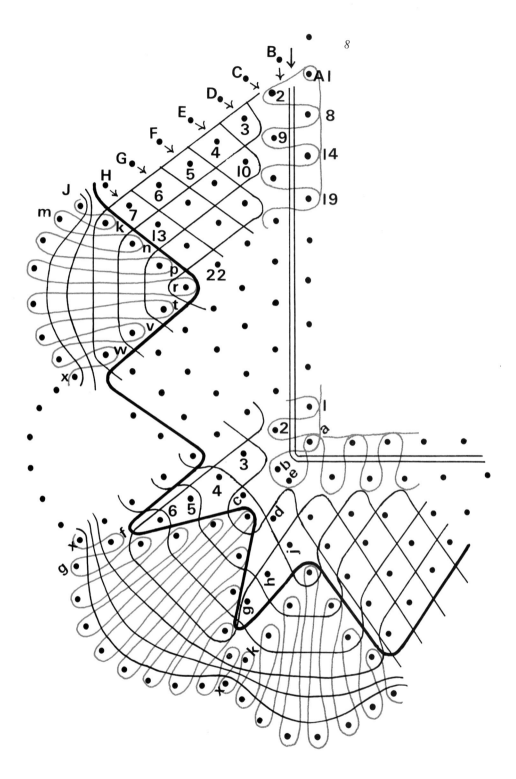

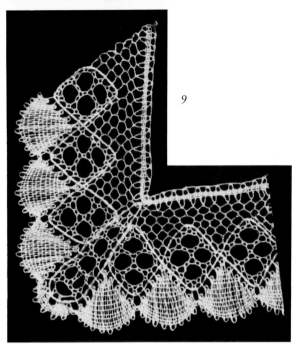

9

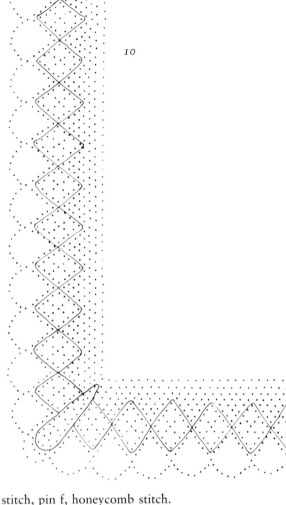

10

Pattern 2. Duke's Garter. Photograph 9.

Prepare nineteen pairs of bobbins, one gimp pair and pricking 10. Refer to diagram 11.

To begin: Place pins in the diagonal row of holes A to J.

Hang two pairs round pin A, two pairs side by side on pin B and one pair on each pin, C to J.

Footside and ground: Follow the instructions for the previous pattern, but work one ground stitch extra using the pair from J for pin 8. Work five rows of ground altogether, stopping at pin 9. Remove support pin B and ease the pairs into position.

Honeycomb diamond: Replace pin J and on it hang the gimp pair. Hang one pair on each pin K to O. Take the right-hand gimp thread to the right through five pairs from the ground. Take the left-hand pair through the five pairs on support pins. Twist all pairs twice.

Pairs from K and 8 work honeycomb stitch, put up pin a between the pairs and work a honeycomb stitch with the same pairs to cover the pin.

Pairs from L and the left from a work a honeycomb stitch, pin b, honeycomb stitch.

Pairs from M and the left from b work a honey-comb stitch, pin c, honeycomb stitch.

Pairs from N and c work d, and from O and d work e.

Remove support pins J to O.

Pairs from a and the ground work honeycomb stitch, pin f, honeycomb stitch.

Pairs from b and c work pin g and pairs from d and e work pin h.

Note that honeycomb pins a to e are linked, a pair travelling from one pin to the next. This is known as a *continuous* row. Pins f, g and h are worked independently, there is no connection between these pins and reference is usually made to a *gap* row.

Work the continuous row from j to o. Begin with pairs from f and the ground for pin j.

Work the gap row p, q, r.

Work the continuous row s to w.

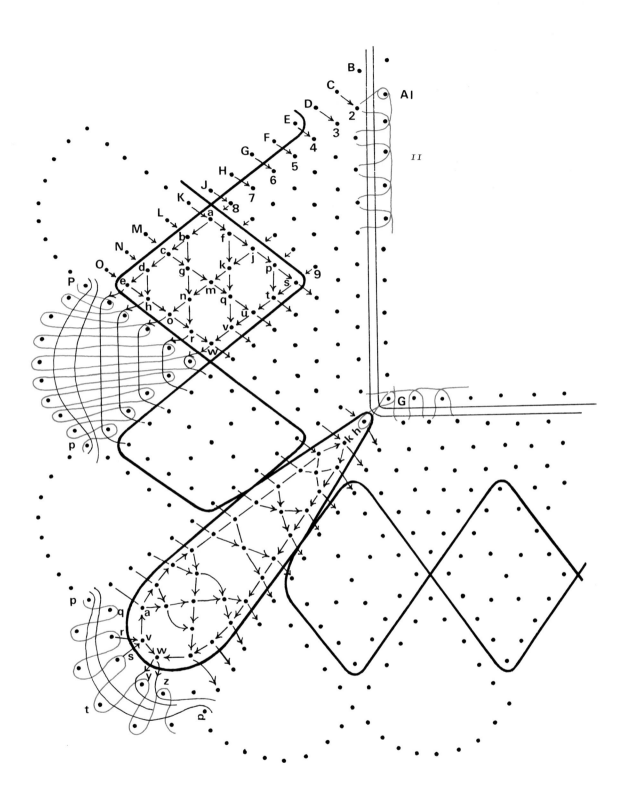

II

The gimp thread at e passes to the right through five pairs, under and over threads of each pair. The gimp thread at s passes to the left over and under the threads of each pair. Cross the gimp threads right over left.

Twist threads from e to w twice each in preparation for the cloth fan. Twist the pairs from s to w three times in preparation for the ground.

To work the fan: Hang three pairs on pin P. The left-hand pair is the weaver which works three cloth stitches through the two pairs on P and one from e.

Complete the fan. If necessary refer to the previous pattern.

One pattern repeat is complete.

Order of work: Many simple patterns can be worked logically in sections. This is a good example of where it is possible to work ground, honeycomb, fan, completing each section before starting the next.

The corner

Two extra pairs are required.

On the footside, work pin G as a normal footside pin using the fourth pair from the edge, the weaver travels back through the two passive pairs and waits to be included in honeycomb later.

On the headside, take the weaver from p and work through two cloth pairs only, put up pin q, return to the outside edge and back through two pairs. Hang two pairs on support pin a and take the weaver through one of these pairs. Put up pin r, return to the outside edge and back through two cloth pairs. Ignore the pair taken in at pin r but take in the second pair from a before putting up pin s. Remove the support pin a and pull down the pairs which should hang at r and s. Take the weaver back to t.

Pairs from r, s, the fan, the honeycomb and ground are brought round the gimp thread for the corner honeycomb. Twist all pairs twice. There are no twists between gimp threads.

Pairs from s and r work honeycomb pin v. The right-hand pair continues to make a continuous row of honeycomb stitches as far as k. The gap row or independent pins are worked as shown in the diagram. The left-hand pair from k works a continuous row back to w.

Note that the weaver from the footside G works the honeycomb pin h independently, it is not linked to k. Bring the gimp threads to meet and overlap

through the five pairs shown in the diagram.

The right-hand pair from h will return to work another footside pin at G later.

On the headside the weaver from t travels through three pairs in cloth stitch to take in one pair from w before pin y is put in position. It returns to the outside edge and back through four pairs, pin z is put up and weaving continues. The extra pairs are discarded one at a time. To do this, lay a pair back and weave on omitting them from the cloth stitch. The cloth stitch will close up and later they can be cut off close to the work. Knots are unnecessary.

Work the fan from p.

Work the honeycomb diamond.

To work the ground, make a ground stitch with the pair from the right side point of the diamond and pin k. Complete the diagonal row.

Work the next diagonal row from h.

Work the corner footside pin G and proceed normally.

Pattern 3. Photograph 12.

This narrow edging can be made very quickly and is an excellent pattern on which to practise picots. A full explanation of the method for making picots is given after the general instruction for this pattern.

Prepare eleven pairs of bobbins and one gimp pair. Prepare pricking 13 and refer to diagram 14.

To begin: Hang two pairs on pin A, two pairs in order on B and one pair on each pin C to E.

Footside and ground: Work from A1 to 4 and from 5 to 7. If necessary refer to the fan pattern. Remove support pins C, D and E.

Hang the gimp pair on E and pairs on F and G.

Cloth four pin bud: Take the right-hand gimp through pairs from 4 and 7. Take the left-hand gimp through two pairs from F and G. Twist all pairs twice.

Pairs from F and 4 work a cloth stitch, put up pin a between them. Twist the left-hand pair twice and work two cloth stitches to the right. Put up pin b to the left of the weaver. Twist the weaver twice.

Weave to the left with three cloth stitches, put up pin c to the right of the weaver. Twist the weaver twice.

Weave to the left through two pairs. Put up the pin d to the left of the weaver. Twist the weaver twice and cover the pin with cloth stitch.

Remove pins E, F and G.

Twist each pair twice and bring the gimps to cross

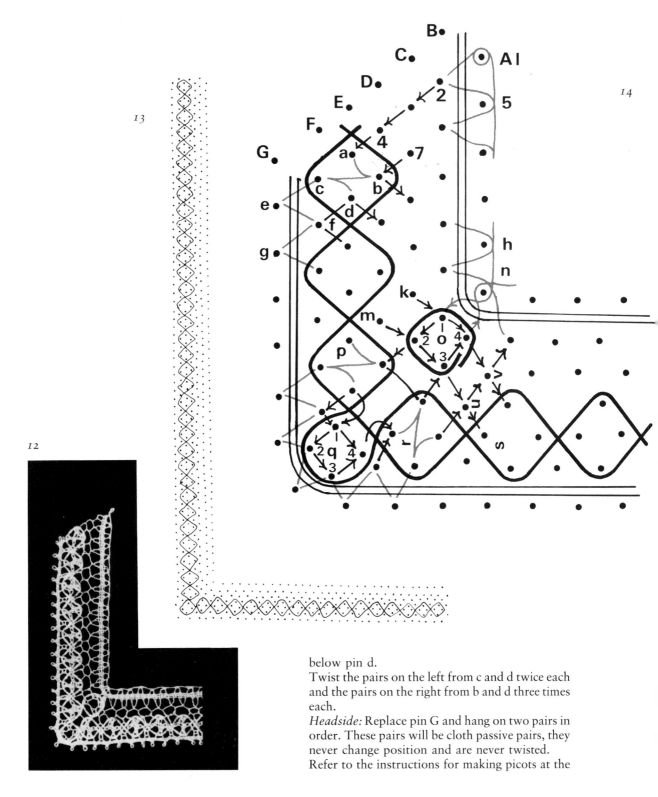

below pin d.

Twist the pairs on the left from c and d twice each and the pairs on the right from b and d three times each.

Headside: Replace pin G and hang on two pairs in order. These pairs will be cloth passive pairs, they never change position and are never twisted.

Refer to the instructions for making picots at the

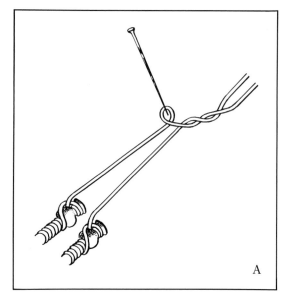

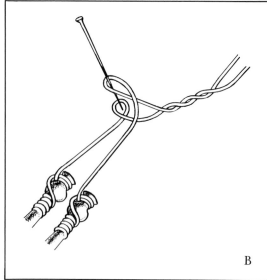

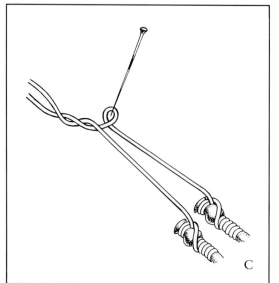

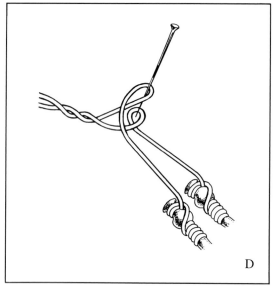

end of this pattern.

The pair from c works cloth stitch through the two pairs on G. Twist the weaver three times, make the picot, twist the weaver three times, and work cloth stitch back through the same passive pairs on G. Twist the weaver twice.

The weaver from picot e and the pair from d work a honeycomb stitch, pin f, honeycomb stitch.

The left-hand pair from f works two cloth stitches to the outside edge.

Twist the weaver three times, make picot g, twist three times, work cloth stitch back through the passive pairs, and twist twice.

The left-hand gimp passes through the pairs from f and g, twist the pairs twice.

One pattern repeat is complete.

The corner

One extra gimp pair is required.
Work the footside and ground from h to m.
Work the footside (corner) pin n and bring the weaver back through two passive pairs. Place the new gimp pair through the pairs from m, k and n. The four pin buds o and q are worked with honeycomb stitches, not cloth.
Pairs from k and n work honeycomb pin 1 in bud o. The left-hand pair from 1 and the right-hand pair from m work pin 2.
The pair from m and the pair from 2 pass round the gimps to work bud p in cloth stitch.
Work the headside.
Work bud q using the holes in the order indicated on the diagram in honeycomb stitch. Turn the pillow.
Work bud r in cloth stitch.
Complete bud o in honeycomb stitch.
Work pins u and v and bud s.
Use the corner pin n a second time as in previous patterns.

Picots

Most Bucks Point patterns have headside picots for decoration. Double picots (i.e. those using both threads of the pair twisted on the pin) are correct. Refer to illustration 15 and the written instruction. Picots are simple to make but the explanation appears wordy and complicated.

Picot on the left-hand side (as required for edgings)

Refer to illustration 15 A and B. Twist the pair three times. Take a pin in the right hand with the point towards the lacemaker; pass the pin under and over the outside thread and, leaving the thread very loose about the pin, put the pin in the picot hole. Now pass the inner thread about the same pin, loosely and in a clockwise direction. Twist the pair three times and pull firmly, inclining the pair well to the right so that the threads 'cord' together around the pin.

Picot on the right-hand side (as required for decorative lengths, circles and oval shapes)

Refer to illustration 15 C and D. Twist the pair three times. With the point of the pin towards the lacemaker, take the pin under and over the outside thread loosely. Take the inner thread round the pin in an anticlockwise direction. Twist the pair three times and pull together to 'cord' the threads around the pin and make the picot.
When pins are removed sometimes the picot splits into two threads. To avoid this keep both threads very loose about the pin and pull up at the same time.
Practice is required.

Pattern 4. Cat's Face. Photograph 16.

A well-known pattern, this combines the features learnt in patterns 2 and 3.
Prepare sixteen pairs of bobbins, a gimp pair and pricking 17.
Refer to diagram 18.
To begin: Work five rows of footside and ground starting at pin A1. Stop at pin o.
Honeycomb: Pass the gimp through four pairs from the ground, but not through the pair from pin o. On the headside hang four pairs on support pins and pass the gimp through these pairs. Twist all eight pairs twice each.
The honeycomb arrangement is similar to that in pattern 2, but the side pins p and q lie outside the gimp. Work continuous row from k to u.
Hang the two passive headside pairs on a support pin to fall on the left of the other bobbins.
To work pin p take the left-hand pair from u out round the gimp and twist twice.
Work two cloth stitches through the passive pairs and twist three times. Make the picot at p and twist three times to complete the picot. Work cloth stitch back through the two passive pairs, twist twice, and pass round the gimp. Twist twice and with the pair from u work honeycomb pin v.
To work pin q take the right-hand pair from r round the gimp to the right.
Twist three times and work a ground stitch with the pair from o. Take the left-hand pair from q back round the gimp and twist twice for honeycomb. Use the pair from r for honeycomb pin s. Complete the honeycomb and enclose it with gimp, cross the gimp threads right over left.
Headside: Work picot pin x and using the pairs indicated in the diagram work honeycomb pin y. Work picot pin z.
Cloth stitch bud: Refer to the diagram and work the cloth stitch bud as in pattern 3.

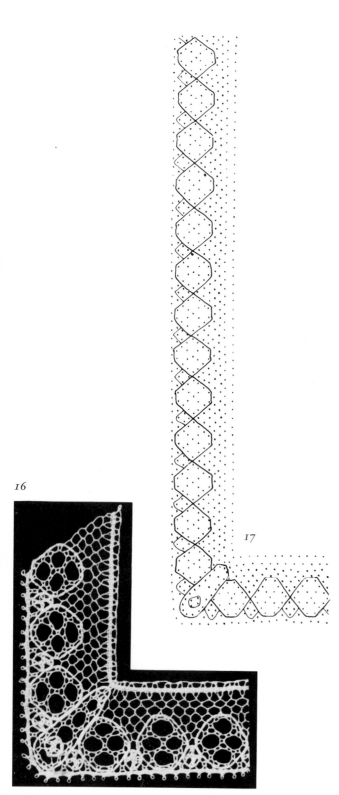

16

17

Headside: Work as for xyz.
One pattern repeat is complete.

Corner

This is similar to pattern 2. Two pairs extra are required.
At the ringed dot make a false picot by placing two pairs round the pin, twisting each pair three times and working a cloth stitch. Twist each pair twice. Use the right-hand pair and work cloth stitch through the passive pairs. Make a cloth stitch with the two outside pairs. Take the third pair from the edge, work two cloth stitches to the edge and a picot into the next pin. Work back through two passive pairs. Place the gimps as shown in the diagram.
Work honeycomb pin a and continue the honeycomb working to the right to z. Work the four pin cloth bud, enclosed by gimp and the gap row stitches. Complete the honeycomb from z to b. Enclose with gimp. Pairs from b work the next two picot pins. Remember to discard the extra pairs in the headside passive trail.
Work the cloth bud and the honeycomb. Continue.

Pattern 5. Photograph 19.

A simple pattern included to describe the method used for the curved headside in Bucks Point lace, it can be worked with or without a tally. The honeycomb feature is identical with that used in Cat's Face and the pattern should be made to practise the heading.
Prepare sixteen pairs of bobbins, one gimp pair and pricking 20.
Refer to diagram 21.
To begin: Work footside and ground, and honeycomb referring to the previous pattern if necessary. upv and rqs are labelled as in diagram 18. Enclose the honeycomb with the gimp threads and cross right over left.
The picot head: The pair from v works cloth stitch through two passive pairs to work picot V. Work two cloth stitches back through the two passive pairs.
The pair from w works cloth stitch through all passives to the outside edge, makes picot W and works cloth stitch back through TWO pairs only. Do not twist.
Similarly the pair from x travels to the outside edge, makes picot X and travels back through

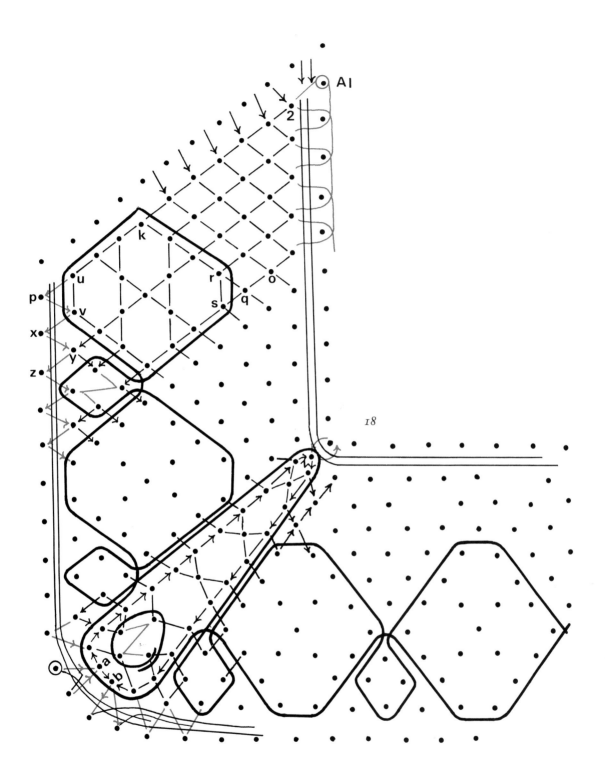

A1

2

p

x

z

y

u

v

k

r

s

o

q

18

a

b

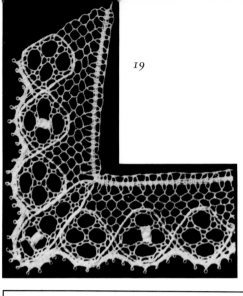

19

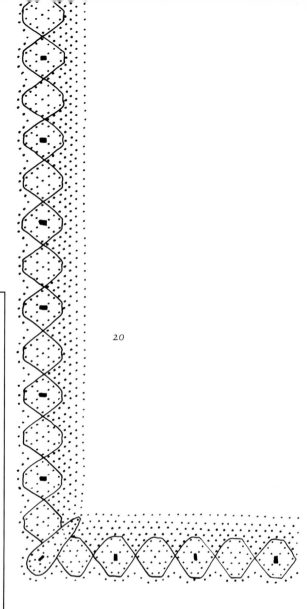

20

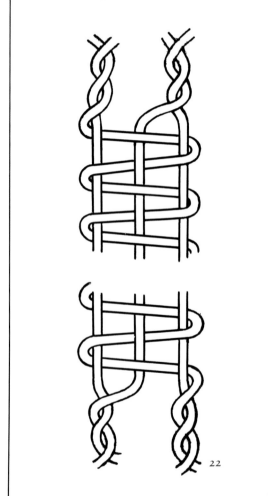

22

TWO pairs only. The pair from y travels to the edge, works picot Y – note the position – and back through two pairs.

Study this carefully and ascertain that all the pairs from the honeycomb have been used for picots. Also, when the honeycomb is worked in the next repeat the pair from u will work p. So there is only one picot to be made to prepare for the honeycomb. The pair from Y has travelled back through two passive pairs, continue through one more and use this pair to make the last picot. Take it out to the edge through the two pairs, make picot Z and

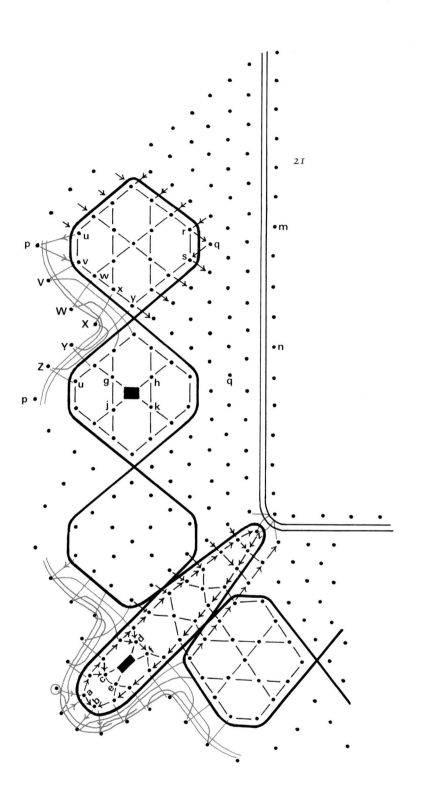

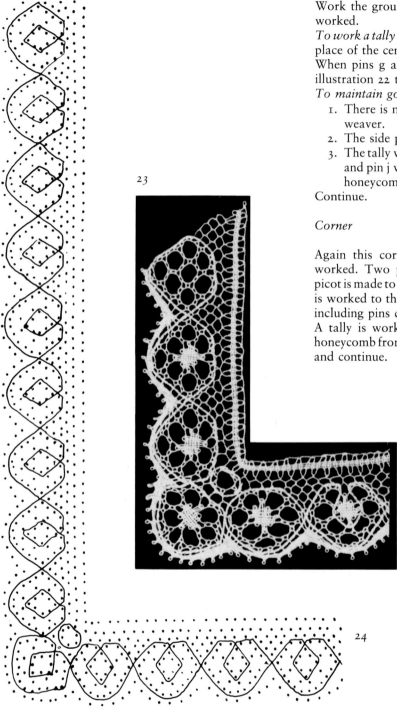

come back through two pairs only.

Pass the gimp thread through the four pairs for the honeycomb.

Work the ground from m to n, q is the last pin worked.

To work a tally in honeycomb: The tally is made in place of the centre stitch.

When pins g and h have been worked, refer to illustration 22 to make the tally.

To maintain good shape ensure that:

1. There is no unnecessary pulling of the tally weaver.
2. The side pairs are taut throughout.
3. The tally weaver is left on the right-hand side and pin j worked before pin k. Complete the honeycomb and enclose with gimp threads.

Continue.

Corner

Again this corner is similar to others already worked. Two pairs extra are required. A false picot is made to supply pairs for pin a. Honeycomb is worked to the right to z. A gap row is worked including pins c and d.

A tally is worked from cd to ef. Complete the honeycomb from z to b. Enclose with gimp threads and continue.

23

24

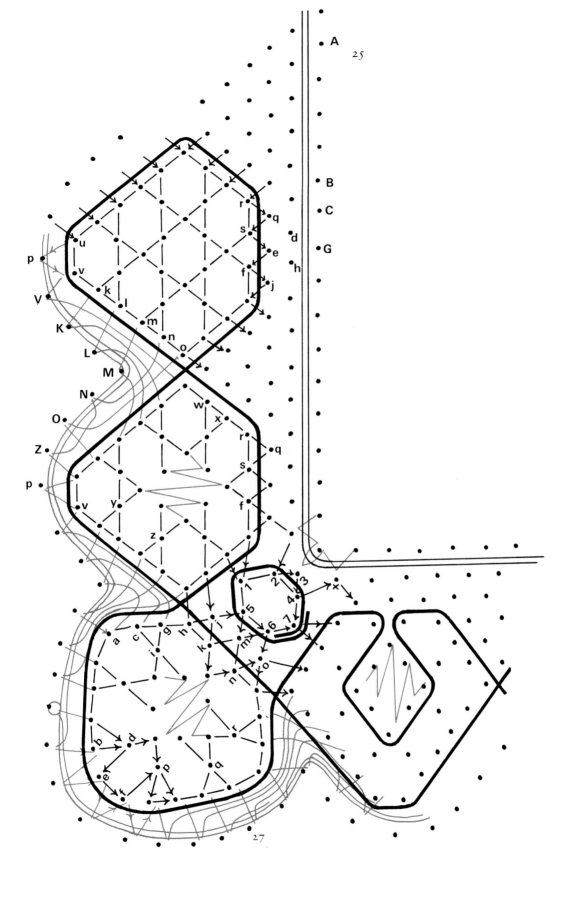

25

27

Pattern 6. Photograph 23.

The photograph and diagram illustrate the lace worked in three different ways.

The first method explains the working for basic honeycomb filling. In the second a cloth diamond – known as 'mayflower' – is worked in the honeycomb and in the third this is surrounded by a gimp thread. The pricking has the gimp marked for the third method.

Prepare seventeen pairs of bobbins, one gimp pair and pricking 24.

Refer to diagram 25.

To begin: Work the footside and ground from A to B.

Honeycomb: Work honeycomb as in previous patterns. Work upv and rqs as in diagram 18. Complete the continuous row from s to m. Take the pair from s round the gimp thread, twist three times in preparation for ground.

Work footside and ground from C to e. Remember to start with the fourth pair from the edge and work out to C, back to the catch pin d and on to ground pin e.

Take the left-hand pair from e round the gimp and twist twice.

Work the gap row from f to n. Take the pair from f out for the ground.

Work G to j as C to e.

Complete the honeycomb. Enclose with the gimp threads and cross them below o.

Headside: The principle applied is the same as that used in pattern 5.

Take each pair from the honeycomb to the outside edge to make a picot and return through two pairs only. The small letter used to indicate the honeycomb relates directly to the capital letter used for the picot.

Picot pin Z is worked as described in the previous pattern. (The pair making picot O travels back through three pairs and the third passive pair then travels to the edge to make picot Z and back through two pairs.)

One repeat is complete.

Honeycomb with mayflower: To work a mayflower it is necessary to understand honeycomb. Work the first continuous row and the gap row from w to v.

Work the first two pins only in continuous row from x, work r and s.

Isolate the six pairs needed for the cloth diamond. *Never* work the mayflower until all the pairs are available. Work the diamond in cloth stitch and then twist each pair twice. Complete the continuous rows from y and z and the gap row from f. Work the last continuous row to complete the honeycomb.

Honeycomb and gimp enclosed cloth diamond: Prepare for the cloth diamond as described above, isolate the pairs. Take the right-hand gimp thread through these pairs, twist the pairs twice and work the cloth diamond. Twist the pairs twice and take the same gimp thread below the diamond through the pairs, twist pairs twice more and continue as described above.

Corner

The gimp thread may be used as shown in the diagram or as in the pricking accompanying these instructions. Two pairs extra and a gimp pair will be required. Work footside and ground to the corner pin, and bring the weaver back through the two passive pairs. Following the diagram introduce a new gimp pair and work the circle from pins 1 to 4.

On the headside work a false picot and the next picot required for b.

Take the gimp thread through sufficient pairs to work honeycomb row ab.

Work the picot pin in preparation for pin e. Complete the gap row from c to d and e. Work the next picot pin in preparation for pin f. Work honeycomb pin f and the next picot. Work pins g, h and i. Pin j is worked as q in the basic instructions. Work k and the mayflower. Complete rows from p and q.

Work pin 5, pin m, pin n and pin 6. Work pin o and the honeycomb can be completed.

Work pin 7 and enclose the ring with gimp threads, these are no longer required.

Use the corner pin a second time and work catch pin x. Work the picot heading discarding the two pairs no longer needed.

Pattern 7. Photograph 26.

Prepare sixteen pairs of bobbins, one gimp pair and pricking 27.

Refer to diagram 28.

To begin: Work the footside and ground rows from A to C, ground pin c is the last pin worked. Hang a gimp pair on a support pin behind the work and pass the right-hand thread through pairs on

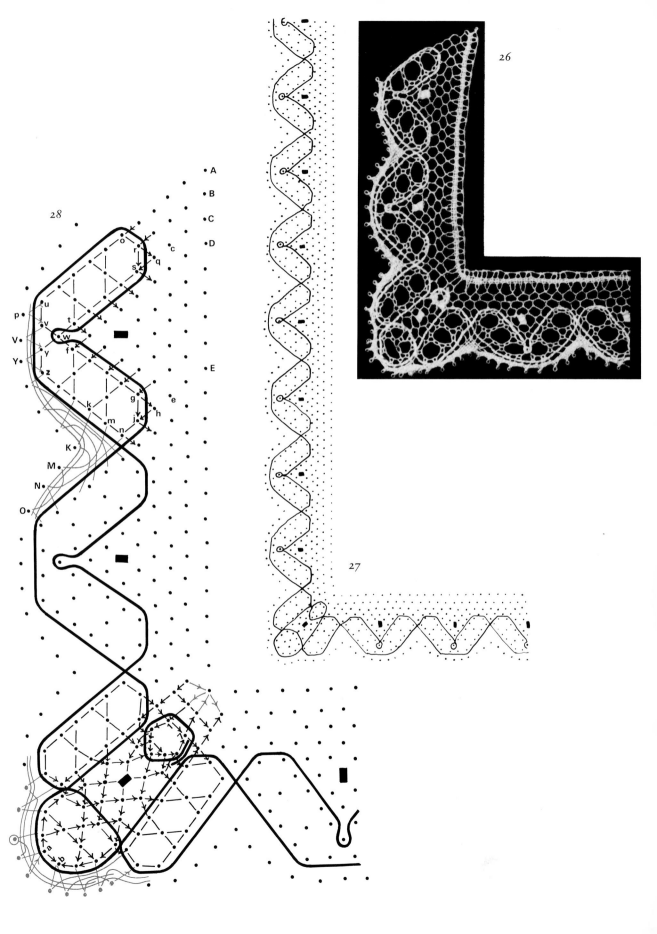

26

28

A
B
C
D

c

q
r
s
o

p
u
V
v
t
Y
w
f
y
z

K
M
N
O

E

e
g
h
k
j
m n

27

the diagonal from A and B. Hang six pairs on support pins on the headside and take the left side gimp through these pairs. Twist pairs twice.

Honeycomb: This is worked in two parts as the ground must be worked to supply the pairs for the second part from y. Work the continuous honeycomb row from o to u. Work the gap row from r and picot p and pin v. Work pin q and the continuous row from s as far as t. Bring the right-hand gimp thread through the pairs from s to t. Twist pairs three times ready for ground. Take the gimp on through the left-hand pair from t and the right-hand pair from v. Twist each pair twice and work honeycomb pin w. Take the gimp to the right through these two pairs, work pins V, y, Y and z.

Ground: Work rows from D to E, the last pin worked is pin e. The tally is made as described on page 24. Note that the tally is worked instead of the ground stitch and the pairs available for the stitch work the tally.

To complete the honeycomb: If it appears to be easier, the lacemaker can work diagonally from right to left as usual. However, with practice, most people will work from f to g. Pin h is worked as pin q. Work the gap row down to j. Complete the last continuous row from z to n. Cross the gimp threads below n.

Headside: Take each honeycomb pair in turn out to make a picot and bring it back through two passive pairs only. Note that pin k works to picot K, m to M and n to N. From N the pair travels back through three pairs and then the third pair from the edge travels out to work pin O and returns through two pairs only.

One repeat is complete.

Corner

Two pairs and one gimp pair extra are needed. Make a false picot where indicated in the diagram. Work honeycomb from pin a. In the circle the first pin to be worked is labelled 1, the last pin is 7. Both pairs from b travel out to make picots and two pairs are discarded in the headside cloth trail. Refer to the diagram.

Pattern 8. Photograph 29.

The six pin honeycomb ring is a common feature in Bucks Point patterns and is used frequently in the designs at the end of this book. A simple pattern called 'Pheasant's Eye' used to be very popular for children's clothes. The pricking is included alongside the pricking which is required to work the lace in photograph 29.

Prepare fifteen pairs of bobbins and one gimp pair. Prepare pricking 30.

Refer to diagram 31.

To begin: Work footside and ground rows A, B and C. Remember that pin q cannot be worked until the pair is available from r. Hang a gimp pair

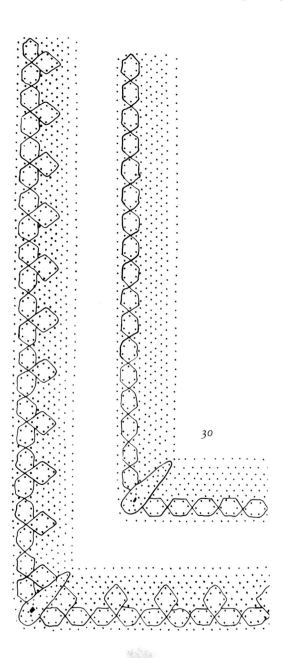

30

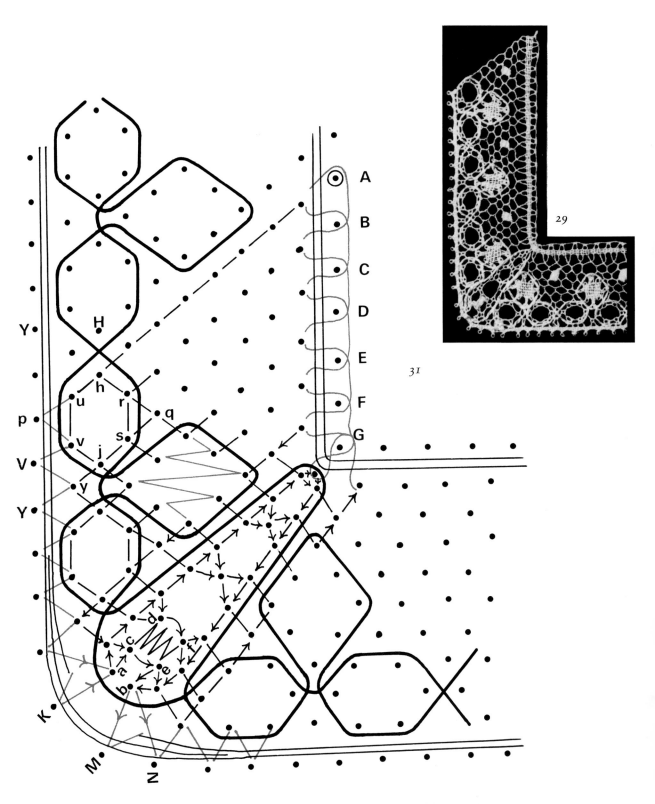

A

B

C

D

E

F

G

H

Y

p

V

Y

K

M

N

31

29

31

on H and two pairs on support pins on the headside. Take the gimp through pairs ready to begin the ring.

Honeycomb ring: Work honeycomb pin h and then r, q and s. Work u, hang passive pairs on a support pin at Y and work pins p and v. Complete the ring with s and j.

Bring the gimps together below pin j and cross them right over left.

Cloth diamond: In preparation work footside and ground rows D, E and F. Take the right-hand gimp to the right through the six pairs required for the diamond, twist pairs twice and work it in cloth stitch. Twist pairs twice, pass the gimp to the left through the same six pairs and cross it over the gimp below j.

Headside: The pair from v works V. Pairs from V and j work honeycomb pin y and the left-hand pair from y works Y. Pairs from y and Y are ready for the next ring, pass the left-hand gimp through, twisting before and after the gimp. Take the right-hand gimp thread through two pairs from the cloth diamond. Continue. Read the corner instructions at least one pattern beforehand.

Corner

One pair extra is required. The principle is the same as for other corners of this type. However only one additional pair is required and this should be hung on a support pin behind the work and incorporated as an extra headside passive, between the existing pairs. Refer to the diagram for detail. The third pair works picot K, thus providing two pairs for pin a.

Work a continuous row of honeycomb stitches from a to the corner as usual.

Work the gap row including c and d. Make a tally to e and f and complete the honeycomb to b. Pairs from b work picots M and N and eventually the third passive is discarded.

Pattern 9. Photograph 32.

More complicated than previous patterns, this design incorporates techniques learned in patterns 1 to 8. In patterns 3 and 4, cloth four pin buds were used but in this pattern the buds are worked in honeycomb stitch. To understand and work the lace, the lacemaker must be prepared to work the diagonal rows from left to right or from right to left and remember always that the rows are worked

toward the lacemaker.

Prepare twenty-one pair of bobbins and two gimp pairs, also pricking 33.

Refer to diagram 34.

To begin: Work the footside and ground row from A in preparation for pin f.

Place a gimp pair and four pairs of bobbins on support pins in preparation for the six pin ring.

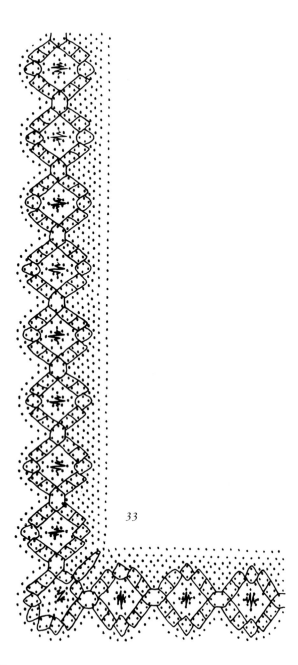

33

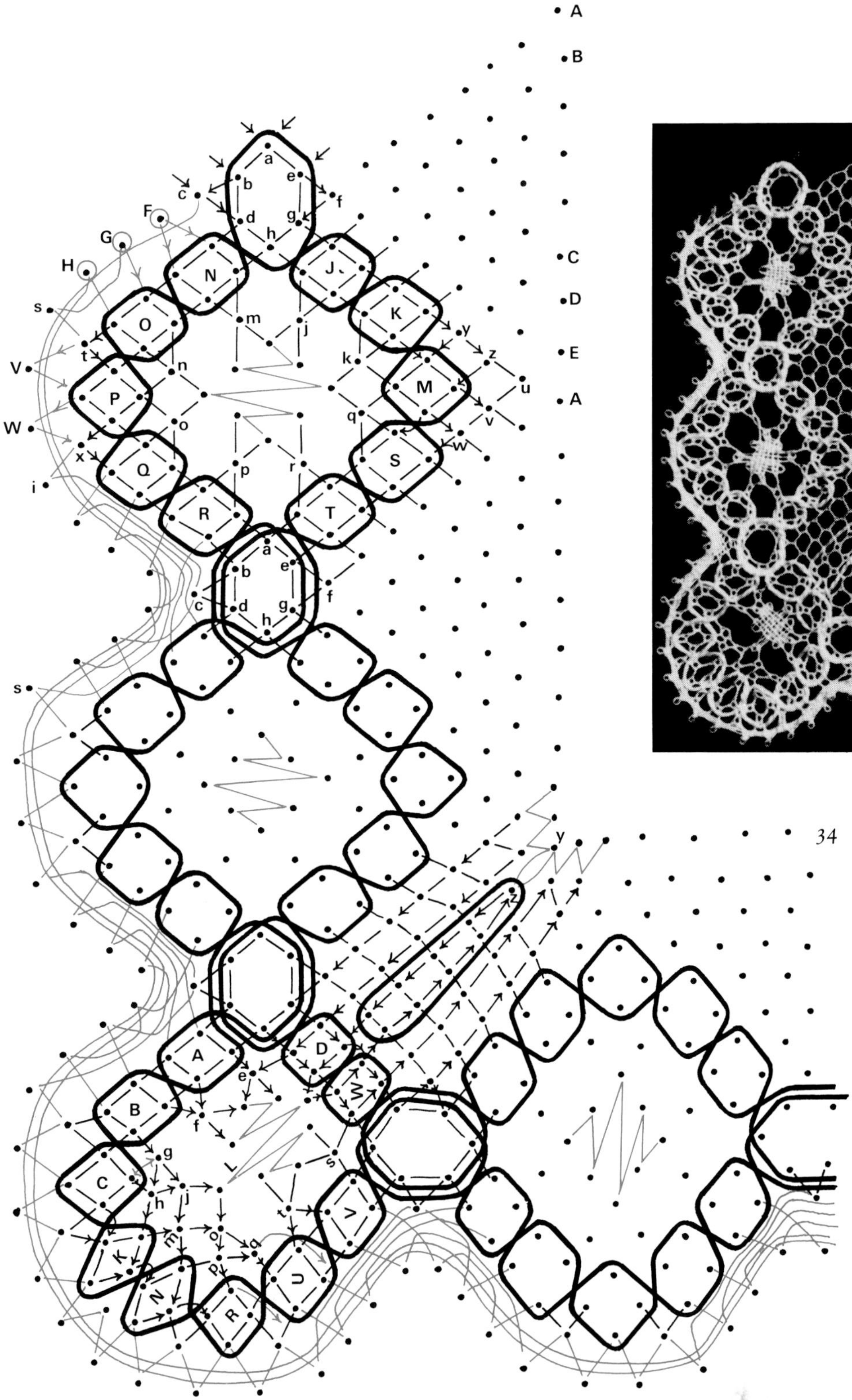
A
B
C
D
E
A
a b c d e f g h
F G H
N O P Q R J K M S T
m j k n o p q r
s t V W x i
y z u v w
a b c d e f g h
s
y
z
A B C D
e f g h j
L
K N R U V W
o p q s t

34

33

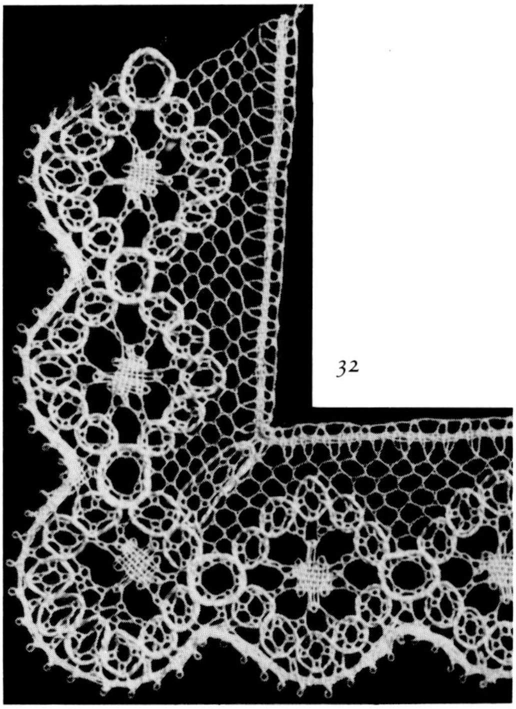

32

Hang one pair on a pin behind c and work false picots at F, G and H and work picot s. Work the six pin honeycomb ring, pins a, b, (c) and d. Then work pins e, (f) and g and finally pin h. Bring the gimp threads together but do not cross them. Place the other pair across the pillow through pairs from d, h and g.

Order of work:

1. Work footside and ground rows from B to E, the last pin worked is E.
2. Four pin honeycomb buds J and K, and N and O.
3. Honeycomb gap row stitches m and n, and j and k.
4. Mayflower.
5. Headside – honeycomb pin t and picot V.
6. Four pin bud P.
7. Headside – picot W and honeycomb stitch x.
8. Ground stitches y and z.
9. Four pin bud M.
10. Honeycomb gap row stitches o and p, and q and r.
11. Four pin buds Q and R.
12. Ground – catch pin u and ground pins v and w.
13. Four pin buds S and T.
14. Honeycomb ring – pins a, b, (c) and d.
15. Footside and ground row from A ready for pin f.
16. Honeycomb ring – pins e, (f) and g. Pin h.
17. Headside picots from i to s.

Corner

Complete the last pattern repeat including the headside and picots.

Footside: Work one more ground row (footside, catch pin and five ground pins.)

Work the corner footside pin y; this pin and pin z are used twice. The pins enclosed by gimp are worked in honeycomb stitch, the first row immediately in preparation for D and the second row back towards the corner after W.

Headside: Refer to the diagram, no extra pairs are required here.

Buds, honeycomb and mayflower: Everything should be worked in letter order A to W.

Note: Pairs are required for C and g. Take two pairs and twist together. The two threads at one end (from different pairs) are passed round the gimp thread, twisted again and used to make the side honeycomb stitch. The other two threads are used for honeycomb stitch g. No longer required

after bud R and pin q the pairs are carried alongside the gimp and discarded below bud V.

Pattern 10. Photograph 35.

Two new techniques are introduced in this pattern, an attractive footside using tallies and known as cucumber foot, also the decorative use of gimp in the ground. The photograph and diagram illustrate different ways of dealing with the finger in the corner.

Prepare twenty-two pairs of bobbins, one pair and one single gimp, also pricking 36. Practice the cucumber foot technique using the pricking 36 but work only the footside and a few rows of ground, refer to diagram 37A.

Cucumber foot

Hang two pairs round pin A and work cloth stitch and twist to cover the pin. Hang two passive pairs on a support pin and take the left-hand pair from A through these pairs as usual in cloth stitch. Twist the weaver three times and put up pin b to the right of the weaver. Take the weaver back through the passive pairs and work footside pin c. Repeat for d and e. Take the weaver back to f, put up pin f and leave ready for the tally. Hang a weaver pair on a pin at g, and work cloth stitch to the left through two passive pairs.

Hang pairs on support pins for the ground. Use the weaver and the next pair to the left to work a ground stitch and put up catch pin h to the right of both pairs. Continue the row of ground normally. Take the pair at h (that is the pair adjacent to the passives) to the right through the two passive pairs in cloth stitch. Put up pin j to the left of the weaver and work back to catch pin k. Continue the row of ground. The pair from k works back through the passive pairs to pin m. Pairs from m and f work a tally. The weaver for the tally will come from the twisted pair at m and it will be discarded in the pair on the right side. Therefore it is important to work the catch pin and ground from n to ensure that the tally retains its shape, before working from f to o. Tallies may be worked at alternate pins, but the inexperienced worker often finds this tedious and slow.

Refer to diagram 37B to work the pattern. The position of the tallies in the footside varies from one pattern to the next. When making the square it is necessary to leave a larger space between or

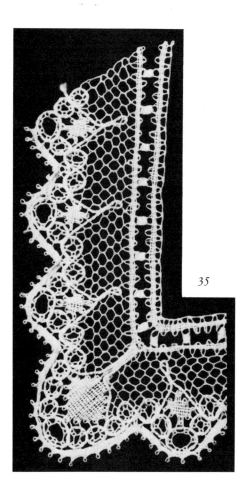

35

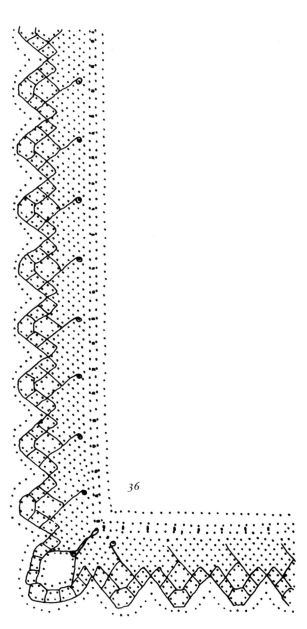

36

work two close together at the corner.

To begin: Work two diagonal footside and ground rows to lead to the four pin bud A.

Hang two pairs on support pins for bud A, arrange gimp threads as shown in the diagram, work bud A in honeycomb.

Hang pairs on support pins and work bud B.

Hang pairs on support pins to work the top three holes, c, g and d of the six pin honeycomb ring.

Hang two more pairs on support pins and work the pair from d out through the passive pairs to picot e, return to work pin f.

Work three rows of footside and ground to h, j and k, and pass the gimp through these pairs.

Work cloth diamond L.

Complete the honeycomb ring with pins m and n.

Work four pin bud O.

To work the gimp finger: Work the ground and put up catch pin y. Take the single gimp thread through pairs from k, w, x and y. Twist pairs from x and y three times each and work ground pin z. Bring the gimp back through pairs from z, w and k. Twist the cloth stitch pairs from the diamond twice each and take the gimp on through these pairs and the pairs from the right-hand side of O. Twist pairs as appropriate and complete the ground row from z. Note that there are no twists between the gimp threads below k and w.

Work one more row of ground and then the four pin bud P.

Picots Q, R, S, T and U are worked in the usual way. The inner passive pair and bottom left-hand pair from P work a honeycomb pin at v.

The left-hand pair from v works picot W, and returns through five passive pairs.

The third pair from the edge works out through two passives for picot X and travels back through four pairs. The third pair from the edge works out for picot Y and back through three pairs. The third pair travels out for picot Z and back through two pairs.

One pattern repeat is complete.

Corner

Four pairs extra are required. Diagram 37B indicates the method, the work should be completed in letter order. When bud Z3 is complete the picots are worked and the four additional pairs discarded gradually in the cloth. Work half of ring R, the cloth diamond S, then complete R.

The working of pins s and t: The pair from catch pin I and the left-hand passive work together in cloth stitch, the gimp thread is passed through both pairs, the weaver from S travels to s and a cloth stitch is made. The weaver travels back through the outer passive, three ground pairs and is ready for pin t.

The gimp passes back through the pair at s, the passive, three ground pairs, the weaver and the pair to the left of it. These pairs work pin t. This method gives a cloth bar across the corner ground. A simpler, though less attractive method is to follow the diagram closely and work as follows.

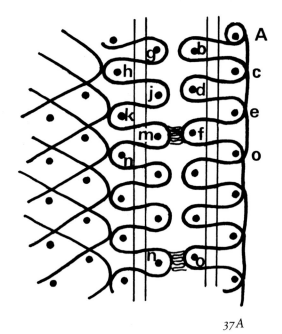

37A

Pin s: Take the gimp through the passive and the pair from pin I. Work a cloth stitch, put up pin s and cover with cloth stitch. Bring the gimp thread back through the pairs and continue. Pin t is worked using the weaver from S and the appropriate ground pair.

Pattern II. Photograph 38.

Prepare bobbins, a gimp pair and a single gimp, also pricking 39.

To assess the number of pairs required

Refer to diagram 40. Count the number of holes in the longest diagonal row, in this case from footside y to picot z, but exclude the picot hole. There are twenty-two holes, add on five, making twenty-seven altogether. The five pairs are needed as follows: one on the footside, and two passives at foot and head. This rule applies to all geometric patterns. However, apart from the convenience of knowing the number of pairs to prepare, there is no merit in the exercise. *A lacemaker will introduce pairs until there are sufficient to work the pattern and to make it look attractive.* Cucumber foot patterns will require an additional three pairs.

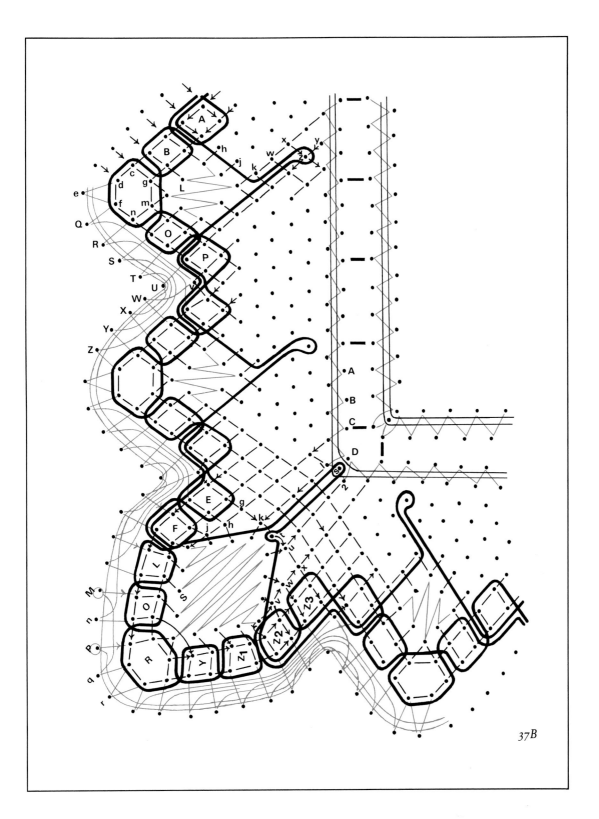

37B

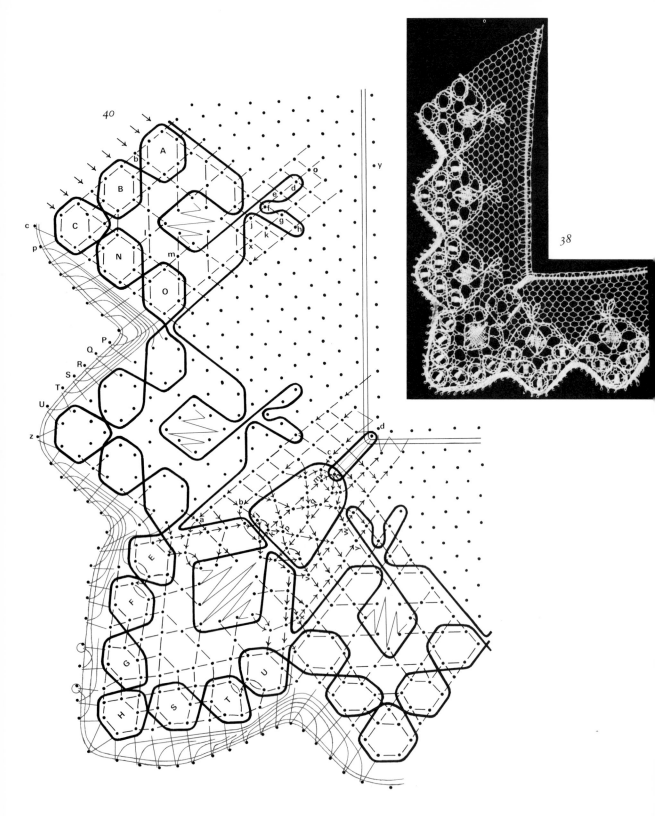

38

To begin: Work seven rows of ground in preparation for the six pin honeycomb ring A and the honeycomb. Always leave the ground on a diagonal line. Work ring A and make b a honeycomb pin. Work rings B and C introducing two passive pairs on the headside before picot c. The honeycomb will provide the pairs for cloth diamond, if necessary refer to pattern 6. Bring the gimp back to the right for the gimp fingers.

To work the gimp fingers: Work three rows of ground leaving them on a diagonal line from o. Take the gimp through the ground pairs including the pair from o and work ground pins d and e. Bring the gimp to the left through four pairs and work pin f. Take the gimp to the right through four pairs to work pins g and h. Bring the gimp through five pairs to the left to work pins j and k.

To complete the pattern feature: Work the honeycomb gap row from j and the continuous row. Remember to work pin x before completing this row. Work pins ı and m and the rings N and O. Do not work the picots until ring O has been completed.

To work the picots: Work picot p and take the pair back through the two passive pairs in cloth stitch. Continue to make picots, each time bringing the pair back through two passives only. Picot P is made with the bottom pair from ring O, this pair travels back through seven pairs (two passives and sufficient for the remaining five picots). The third pair from the edge makes picot Q and this pair travels back through six pairs. The third pair makes picot R and travels back through five pairs. Continue until picot U is worked and the pair travels back through the two remaining passive pairs.

One pattern repeat is complete.

The corner

Follow the diagram and work in letter order. Five pairs extra are required. Note that the odd pair is introduced as an additional passive as in pattern 8. Work as far as possible before turning the pillow, complete the ground rows to a, b and c, and all the picots necessary for rings E, F, G and H. Turn the pillow to continue.

An additional gimp pair is used for the honeycomb feature beginning at pin j.

When all honeycomb is complete turn the pillow to work diagonal rows of ground towards the footside from v to w and from x to y. Arrows

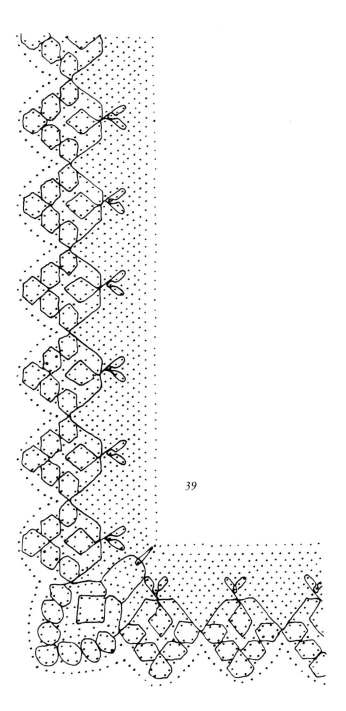

39

indicate the direction in which the pairs travel.
Note: A new gimp is introduced for the cloth bar. Take the pair from n as weaver and make four cloth stitches to the right, support the weaver with a pin in the extra corner hole. Take the weaver back through four cloth pairs and the gimp thread, remove pin n, use the weaver and pair at n to make another honeycomb stitch. Replace the pin and enclose with honeycomb. Overlap the gimp threads, these will be cut off later.

Pattern 12. Strawberry. Photograph 41.

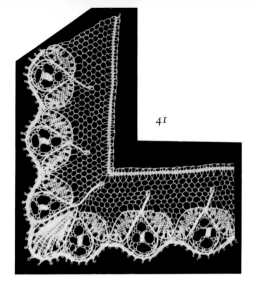

41

Although less geometric in appearance this pattern is worked regularly. Honeycomb pins on the headside require particular care.
Prepare bobbins and one gimp pair, also pricking 42.
Refer to diagram 43.

Order of work

Try to complete each section as far as possible to facilitate understanding and prevent unnecessary movement of bobbins across the pillow.
1. Work the footside and ground from A to B, stop along the diagonal line and work to catch pin b.
2. Introduce the gimp pair through two pairs on support pins and five pairs from the ground.
3. Hang five pairs on a support pin for the headside passive pairs.
4. Work the cloth feature. When the weaver has travelled from c to d, the pair at c works through five passive pairs to make the picot C, and returns for pin e. Weaving continues, bringing in pairs on the right and leaving them out on the left-hand side. The weaver travels from f to g, and the pair at f goes out to work ground pin h. It returns for pin j. Similarly the pair from j will work ground pin m and return for n. Cross the gimp threads below n. Obviously, the ground rows are worked as necessary to provide the pair for m.
5. Work the ground stitches to o and p. Bring the right-hand gimp thread from n through five ground pairs and work ground pin q. Take the gimp back as shown in the diagram.
6. The pair from e and the inner passive work honeycomb pin r. The left-hand pair goes out to work picot R, and travels back through four pairs. The third pair from the outer edge goes out to

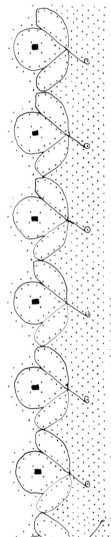

42

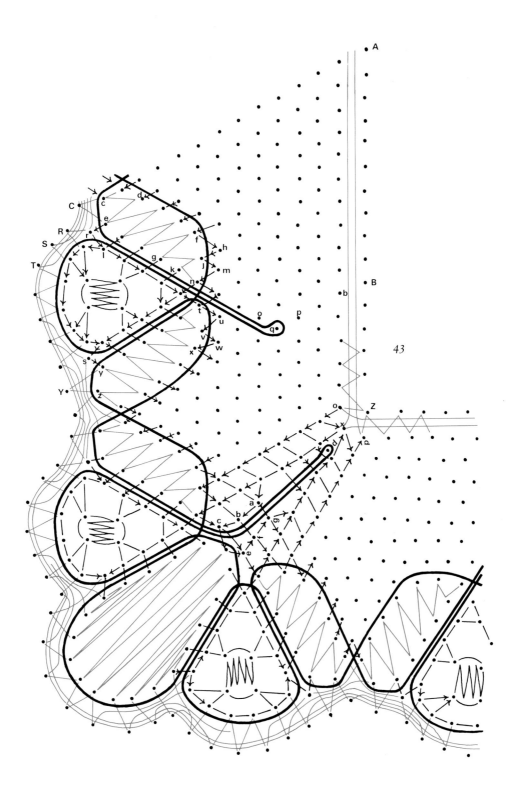

43

41

make picot S, it travels back through three pairs; the third pair travels out for picot T and back through two pairs. The gimp thread can be placed in readiness for the honeycomb feature which begins at pin 1.

7. Work the honeycomb as shown in diagram. Note that the gimp travels all the way round the feature and crosses the other gimp below n.

8. Work honeycomb pin s using the inner passive pair.

9. Work three picots to complete the headside as far as possible.

10. The cloth feature is worked from t. The weaver from t travels to the left, and the right-hand pair goes out round the gimp to work ground pin u. It returns for pin v and goes out again for w. From x one pair is left out after each pin. Note that the pair from y travels out to picot Y and back for pin z.

11. Cross the gimp threads and take the pair from z out to work the next picot, a pattern repeat is complete.

Note: This pattern is regular but it cannot be worked in isolated sections. The honeycomb can be worked as a complete unit, but the cloth is dependent upon the understanding of ground and the working of ground rows and stitches as needed.

The corner

One additional passive pair is introduced on the headside. On the footside the pair from catch pin o works corner footside pin Z and remains there. The inner passive is used to work catch pin x. When the corner is complete the other passive pair works catch pin p and Z is used a second time. It is quite usual to use pins twice in the corner situation and in this pattern both x and Z are used in this way.

Pattern 13. Photograph 44.

This edging has a corner that is particularly easy to understand and to work. The direction of the honeycomb changes across the corner line, which is perhaps less attractive visually but is quick to make.

Prepare bobbins, two gimp pairs and pricking 45. Refer to diagram 46.

To begin: Lace that is joined along a line of gimp thread will be stronger and the join less noticeable, this pattern is started with the cloth diamond and

the ground introduced from pin A. Hang a gimp pair on a support pin and five pairs of bobbins on either side. Work the cloth diamond from a to b. *Hole in cloth:* Work in cloth from b to c through three pairs only (four are left hanging) and work to d and back to e. Put up pin e and leave the weaver hanging to the right of the pin. Remember to introduce a new pair at d. Return to f.

Place pin f between the first and second of the hanging pairs. The pair to the left becomes the new weaver, weaving to g and back to h. Pin h is put up to the right of the weaver and it weaves back to j. Remember to introduce a new pair at pin g and leave out a pair before j. From j to k the weaver passes through seven pairs. Continue to m.

To begin the footside: Hang two pairs on pin A and cover with cloth stitch and three twists.

Hang two passive pairs on a support pin and take the left-hand pair from A through these in cloth stitch as usual. The pair from g is used for catch pin n. Continue footside and ground to B and o.

Headside buds: Introduce the new gimp pair. Use two pairs from support pins and pairs from d and k to work bud P. Introduce two more pairs and work bud Q.

The left-hand pair from Q works honeycomb pin r with a pair from a support pin.

The left-hand pair from r travels to the left through two more pairs on a support pin to work picot R. It returns through the passive pairs and with the other pair from r is ready for bud V. Note that V cannot be worked until the honeycomb row from s is complete.

Work honeycomb stitches s, t and u.

Clothwork: Follow the diagram. From x take the weaver through three cloth stitch pairs, do not twist it, but pass immediately round the gimp threads and then twist three times. Work the ground stitch and put up catch pin y to the left of both pairs. This helps to maintain good tension in the clothwork. Take the weaver back round the gimp and immediately make the three cloth stitches without twisting the weaver. This ensures that the gimps and cloth lie close together and give a solid appearance. Take the weaver out round the gimp thread without twisting and twist twice ready for honeycomb. Before and after pin z work cloth stitch and two twists to ensure good tension in the clothwork. Continue.

Honeycomb, buds and picots: Complete these, noting that one pair travels directly from V to W to maintain the appearance of the honeycomb.

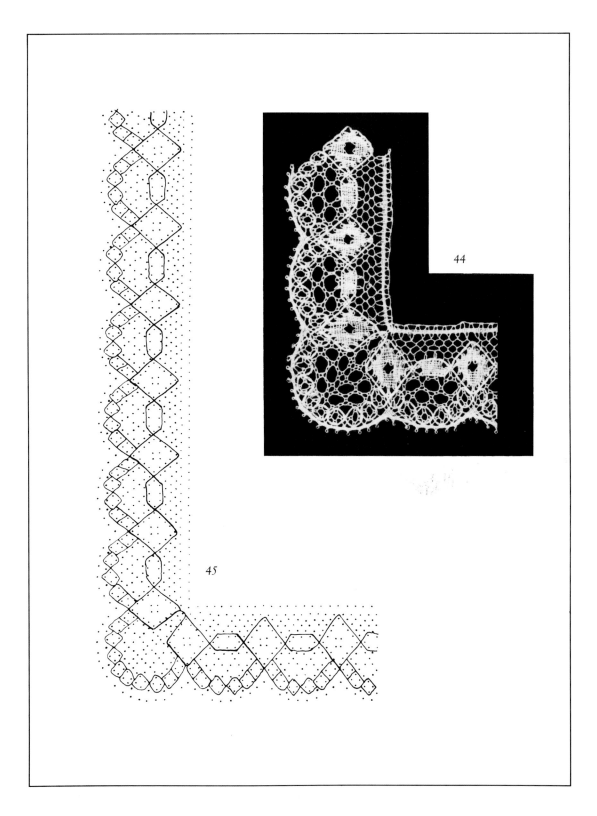

44

45

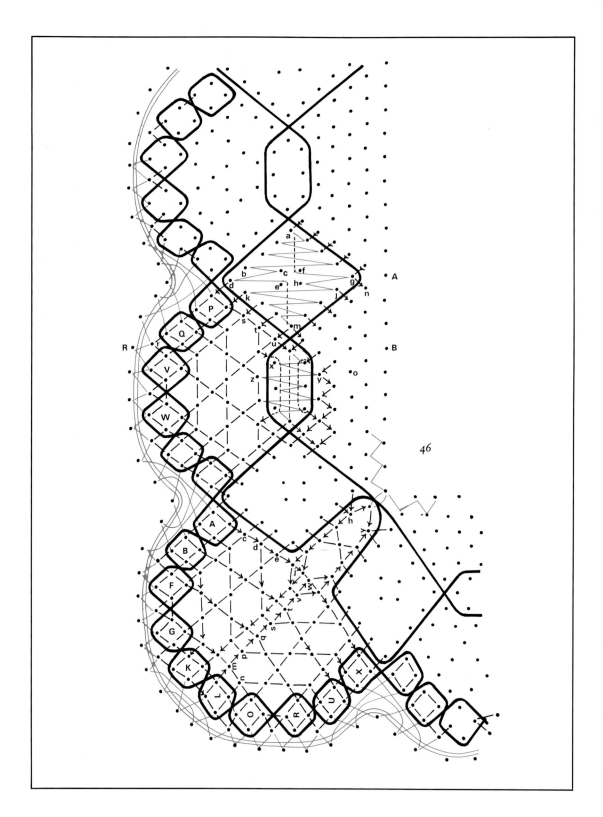

46

The corner

Work buds A and B and honeycomb from c, d and e to provide the pairs for F and G. Begin the honeycomb extension at h and work to j.
Complete the honeycomb gap and continuous rows to work K.
Turn the pillow.
Work L, m, n and O. To work R complete the gap and continuous rows from p and q; for U work rows from s and t; for X work rows from v and w. The honeycomb extension is completed at y.

Pattern 14. Photograph 47.

This pattern appears to be more complicated but the only new feature is the six pin hole in cloth which is described below. Great care and forethought are required to work the holes in the correct order. ALWAYS work the pin holes furthest away first and remember to work diagonally completing rows as necessary.

Advice on working

To begin: Work footside pin A1 and eight ground pins. Work the cloth area B. At the widest part the weaver will travel out round the gimp and make a catch pin stitch as described in pattern 13. From the catch pin the weaver travels back round the gimp thread, through eight cloth pairs including one introduced for pin j. Before placing pin j in position take a gimp thread through the weaver, place the pin between the weaver and the gimp and take the gimp back to the left through the weaver. Continue the cloth stitch area.
When the cloth area B is complete, work from A2 to G in preparation for H.
In position C hang pairs on support pins to work the four honeycomb pins, beginning with the pair from j.
Work area D, at the same time continuing the headside honeycomb and introducing passive pairs and making the picots.
The six pin hole: Refer to the diagram. The weaver at a works to the pair beyond the centre (in this case through three pairs). Put up pin b to the left of the weaver and cover the pin. Both pairs become weavers. On the left side the weaver travels to c where a pair is brought in from the honeycomb, back to d and across to z. Pin z is worked as pin z in

pattern 13. The weaver travels back to e, out to the pin below c and back to f. The other side is worked similarly, but pin y is worked in ground as catch pin. At f the weavers meet, a cloth stitch is worked and the pin covered. One pair hangs as a passive and the other continues as a weaver.

The corner

At m two new pairs are introduced as in pattern 9. At the two pins labelled n there are pairs no longer required. These are carried alongside the gimp thread and eventually discarded.
On the footside the corner pair works pin r to begin the honeycomb feature. This is completed at pin s and the pair returns to use the corner pin a second time.

The Corner

As all Bucks Point patterns are worked along a diagonal line at an angle of 52° or more from the footside there will be difficulty when working a corner.
Torchon lace, worked at an angle of 45° from the footside presents no problem.
Refer to diagram 50. This illustrates the three areas to be worked, the corner area, shaded in the

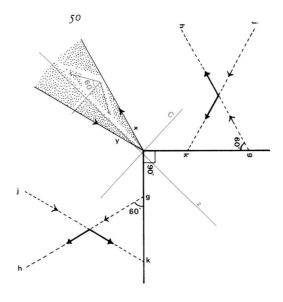

50

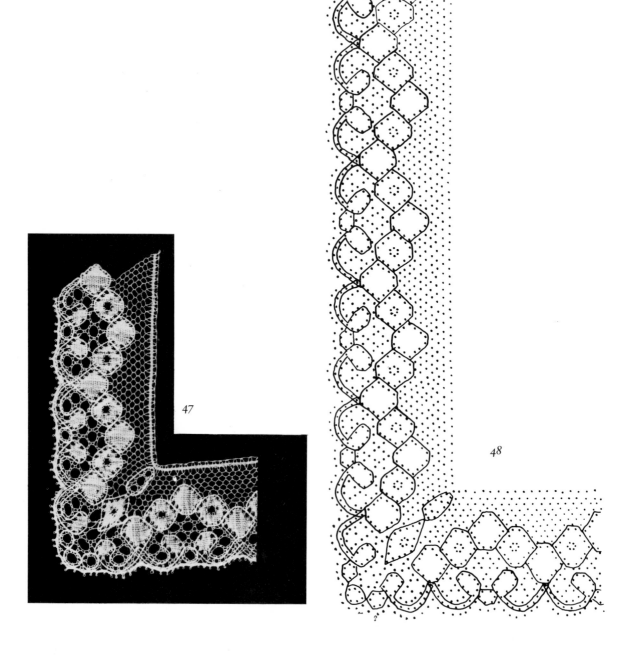

47

48

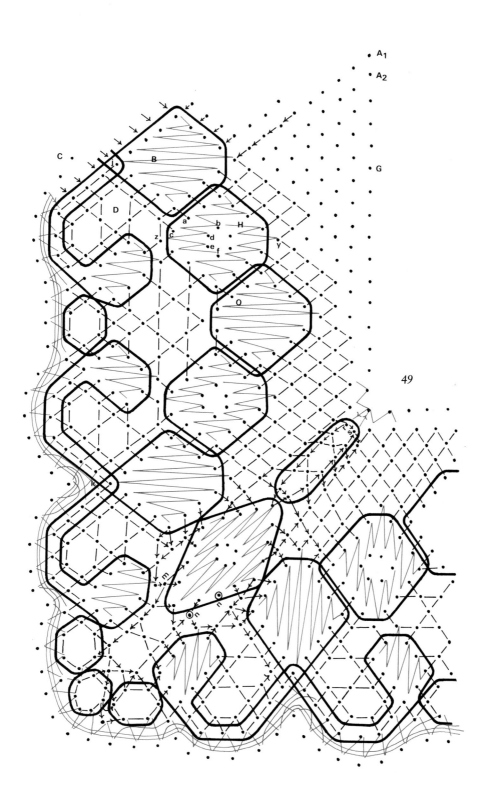

49

diagram, must be worked quite *separately* from the edging before and after the corner. Take the pricking to be worked and diagram 50 and consider the following points:

1. Ground is worked along two diagonal lines, g to h or j to k. It is NEVER worked from h to g or from k to j. The diagonal line x is the last to be worked before the corner. Beyond line x there are no footside pin holes.

2. Turn the pricking and diagram so that the line z is horizontal. Everything within lines x and y is worked with the pillow in this position. The only footside pin is the corner pin but the position of the footside would fall on line c. This is important as it helps the lacemaker to find the diagonal lines for working ground and honeycomb within the corner. Everything within this area must be completed before line y is worked.

3. Turn the pricking and diagram so that the second edge is ready for working. Diagonal line y is in the same position as the line jk. Most lacemakers prefer to work on the line gh. Rows may be worked diagonally from y to the headside in this direction, eventually work proceeds with complete rows from the footside.

Corner designs

There are several popular arrangements used for narrow edgings.

1. The long honeycomb shape enclosed with gimp thread is illustrated in patterns 2, 5 and 8. The honeycomb is usually worked from head to foot and back to the headside. To begin it is important to select a hole where no pair is required for a gap row stitch so that the available pairs remain near the gimp and travel in opposite directions, this occurs at pin v in diagram 11. Occasionally this is not possible; honeycomb pin a in diagram 31 provides pairs for the gap row and the continuous row travelling to the footside.

2. In some narrow designs at an angle of 52° the ground may be enclosed with gimp and worked as a four pin bud. Some adjustment is needed on the headside and another honeycomb bud can be planned and suitable pairs selected to make it look attractive. See diagram 14.

3. The design may be placed across the corner and the ground area adapted to avoid converging rows of holes. See diagram 25.

4. Corners are planned sometimes for ease of working only. In diagram 46, the honeycomb is worked to the corner line, the pillow turned and the honeycomb completed. This cannot look as attractive but is quick to work and simple to understand.

Note: Assess the suitability of available pairs. Never drag pairs out of line as the lace will be untidy and the tension lost. If necessary pairs must be added to make a strong and attractive piece of lace. If an extra pair is required in honeycomb it should be added into the adjoining feature and allowed to enter diagonally. The chief considerations are:
(a) appearance
(b) durability.

Cucumber Foot

This may be added to any pattern. Refer to illustration 51.

A. The normal pricking. Place a piece of clear plastic under the pattern and prick the catch pin and footside rows.

B. Prick the pattern without these two rows of holes. Take the clear plastic and set it in position as shown in B. Pin in position and prick the holes onto the card pricking.

C. Working method.

Note that some adaptation is necessary at the corner when making a handkerchief.

Joining lace

To complete the handkerchief square the join should be strong but not too obvious. In the past lacemakers overlapped the lace by one full pattern repeat but today this is not popular. Pin the beginning of the lace onto the pricking so that the last repeat meets the first and no holes remain unworked. The final position of the pairs is obvious but care is needed to ensure the correct number of twists is given. Refer to illustration 52. Select a position where pairs are joined to cloth, use a small hook to pull one thread through the loop, pass the other thread through the loop formed and pull both threads tightly, tie with a reef knot. Similarly a hook can be passed through a honeycomb stitch or below a ground stitch. When all threads are secure, cut off the bobbins leaving at least four inches (100mm) thread on the lace. The footside thread should be twelve inches (300mm) long.

Lay the threads together along a gimp thread if

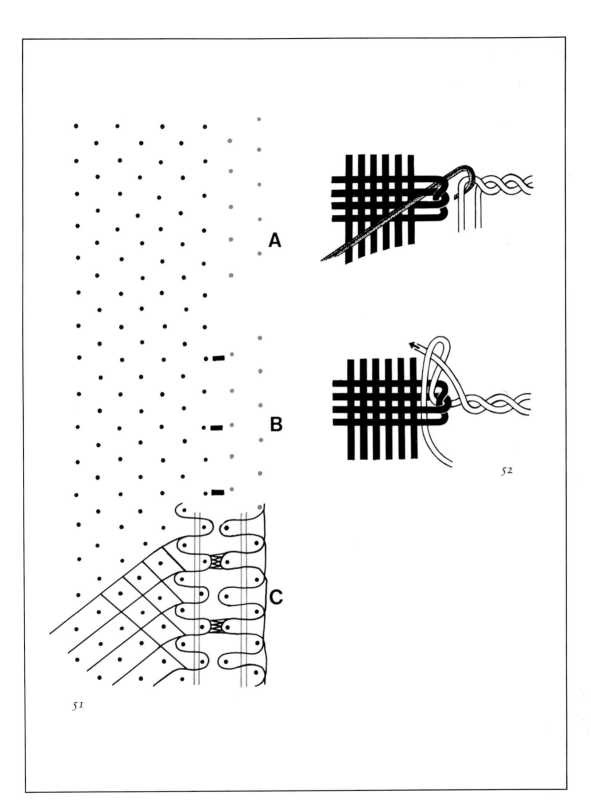

A

B

C

51

52

possible and use the long thread to oversew them firmly onto the gimp or cloth.

Sewing the lace to the linen

Refer to illustration 53. Work on the right side of the fabric. One stitch is made at each footside stitch on the lace. Bring the needle out at A.
Put the needle in at B and out at A (back stitch)
Put the needle in at B and out at A (second back stitch)
Put the needle in at C and out at A
Put the needle in at C and out at D
Put the needle in at C and out at D
Put the needle in at C and out at D
Put the needle in at A and out at D
Put the needle in at A and out at a
There are two back stitches made each time. The footside edge is incorporated into the three sided stitch but the passive pairs remain visible. If the linen fabric is finely woven and the stitches deep enough it should be possible to trim the raw fabric away at the back of the work.

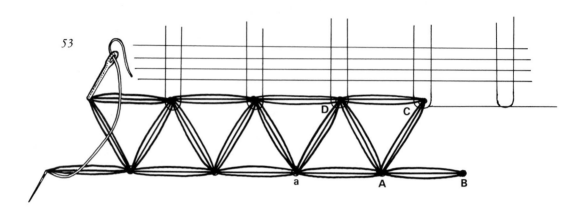

53

four
Decorative Hexagons and Lengths

Today lacemakers want the opportunity to make small pieces of lace that can be used independently and not mounted on fabric. The simplest way to achieve this is to work lace that begins and ends at a point. For decoration, picots are worked on all edges, although it is possible to work a footside if needed.

Pattern 15. Hexagon with Honeycomb and Mayflowers. Photograph 54.

Prepare twenty-four pairs of bobbins, one gimp pair and pricking 55.

Refer to diagrams 56 and 57. The lettering is common to both diagrams.

To begin: Make false picots on pins at A, B and C as follows: Hang two pairs on pin A, twist the threads each side three times each and cover the pin with cloth stitch and two twists. Repeat for pins B and C.

Work cloth stitch using the right-hand pair from B and the left-hand pair from A.

Work cloth stitch using the left-hand pair from C and the right-hand pair from A.

Cross the centre pairs with cloth stitch.

The left-hand pair from B works cloth stitch through two pairs.

The right-hand pair from C works cloth stitch through two pairs.

Twist both pairs twice and pass the gimp through both pairs. Twist to enclose the gimp and work honeycomb pin o.

Note that there are two passive pairs on each side and the gimp which separates these from the honeycomb pairs.

Hang two pairs on D and make a false picot. The right-hand pair travels through two pairs in cloth stitch, is twisted twice, passes round the gimp thread and receives two more twists. Work honeycomb pin p.

The left-hand pair from D and the outer passive work cloth stitch and the third pair from the edge works out through these pairs to make an ordinary picot at e. Working two cloth stitches, two twists, round the gimp, two twists, it is ready for honeycomb pin q. Continue F to r and g to s; H to t and i to u; as described for D to p, and e to q. Before working picot i hang one extra pair on a support pin outside the work and allow it to fall as an additional passive close to the gimp thread. Continue to work picots J, k and L which uses the extra pair, complete the honeycomb as necessary.

On the other side work similarly. When false picot M has been made the gap row is worked. The pair from v goes out to make picot w and returns for honeycomb pin x. When ordinary picot n is made the continuous row of honeycomb is worked, again one pair makes a picot on the left-hand straight side and returns to complete the row.

Mayflowers are explained on page 28.

To complete the work: Finish the honeycomb area and overlap the gimp threads. The pair at pin 1 works out through the passive pairs, makes picot 2 and travels back through two cloth pairs.

The pair from 3 works out to the edge, makes picot 4 and travels back through two pairs only. Similarly the pair from 5 works to the edge and makes picot 6. The inner passive is laid back across the work and ignored, eventually it will be cut off close to the lace. The picot pair travels back through two

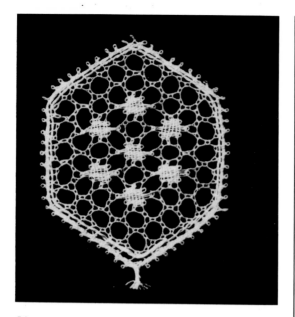

54

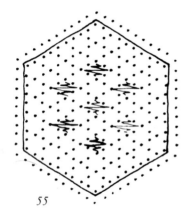

55

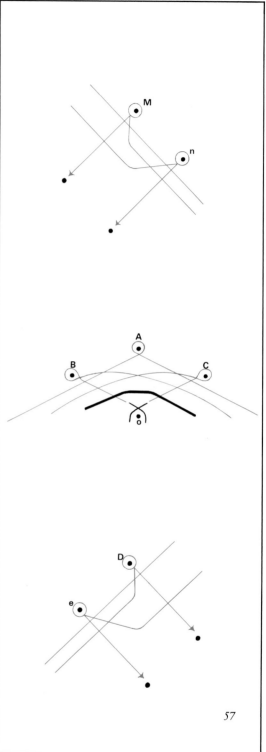

57

only as usual.

Work every pair out to the edge and make picots at the same time discarding the inner passive pair every time.

Ignore hole z. The inner passives are crossed in cloth stitch and taken to the outside edges, bundled around the remaining threads and tied firmly. This can be left as a tassel. The threads discarded are cut close to the work, all bobbins cut off and the pins removed.

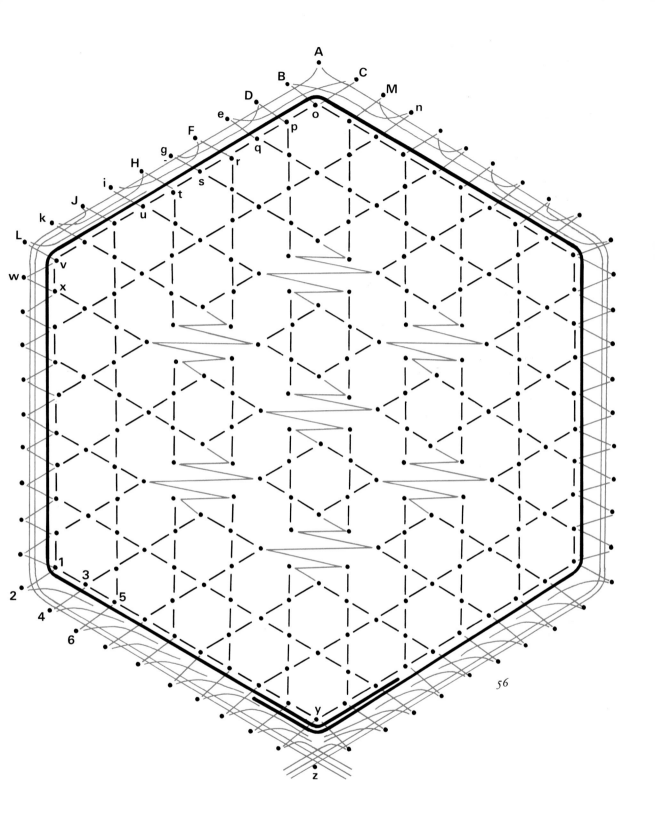

56

53

Pattern 16. Hexagon with Ground and Honeycomb. Photograph 58.

Prepare twenty-four pairs of bobbins, three gimp pairs and pricking 59.

Refer to diagram 60.

The pairs are introduced from false picots as in the previous pattern, the instructions accompanying pattern 15 also apply to diagram 60. However, ground stitches are worked instead of honeycomb. The working of tallies is described on page 26. When three rows of ground have been worked in each direction a gimp thread is introduced and honeycomb pins 1 to 7 are completed. The other side is worked and the third gimp introduced. The honeycomb and mayflower centre is worked.

The vertical row of honeycomb pins within gimp is worked as follows: The left-hand pair from pin 7 passes out round the gimp to work a ground stitch and the right-hand pair goes to the right to work honeycomb. They both come back for pin 8. Remember the gimps must be enclosed with twists, and that pairs in ground always move diagonally, and diagram 60 will be easier to understand.

Pairs from pin 8 are used in ground and honeycomb and return for pin 9. Continue.

58

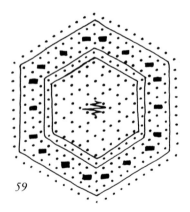

59

54

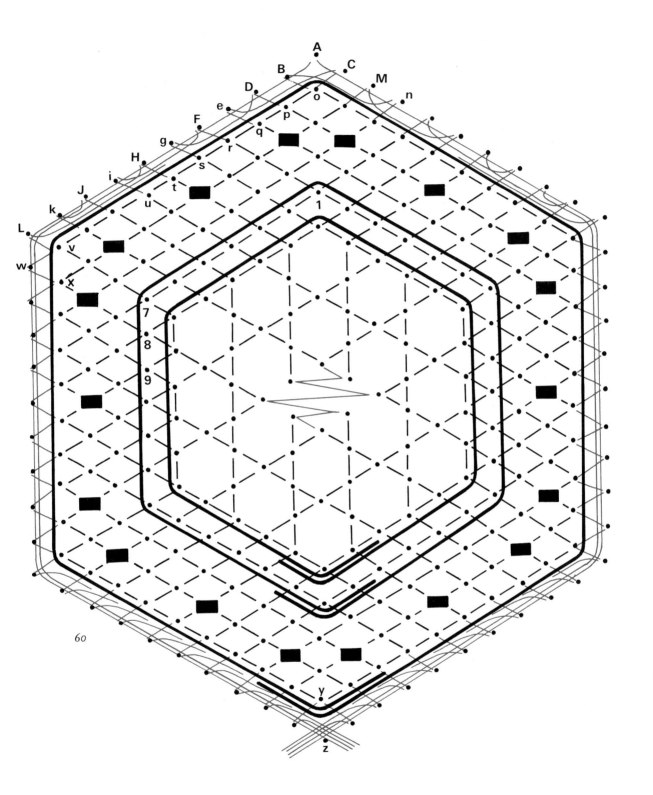

Pattern 17. Hexagon with Honeycomb Rings and Buds. Photograph 61.

Prepare twenty-six pairs of bobbins, four gimp pairs and pricking 62.

Refer to diagram 63.

Pairs are introduced from false picots as in the previous patterns. However, this hexagon is slightly larger and an extra false picot is needed instead of an additional pair introduced into the passives. Introduce one gimp pair and work pins a, b and c in the top ring. The left-hand pair from b passes out to work honeycomb pin d with the pair from picot D.

Returning to the ring pin e is worked. On the right-hand side the pair from c goes out to work honeycomb pin f with the pair from F, it returns for pin g. Complete the ring at h. Introduce the new gimp pair through ten pairs as shown in the diagram, through pairs from K, J, d, e, h, g, f, L, M.

Work ring 2 using pairs from K, J, d and e. The left-hand pair goes out to work honeycomb with the picot pair but the right-hand pair goes into ground working a ground stitch with the pair from the bottom left of ring 1.

Continue to work rings 3 to 7.

Work three ground rows in each direction. Pairs from N, O, O and P pass round another gimp thread to work honeycomb bud 8. Introduce a new gimp through pairs from Q, R, s, t, u, V and W and work bud 9 with pairs from Q, R, s and t. Continue and work bud 10. Work the other side. Work the honeycomb and mayflower. Note that rows of ground are worked before buds 11 and 12.

The bottom six pin ring: The gimp threads from the lower side of the previous rings cross above the last ring. When the side pins have been worked these gimps are discarded to avoid thickness at the bottom. The gimp threads from the tops of previous rings fall on either side of the last ring and enclose it at the bottom.

61

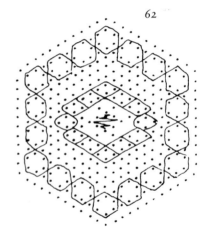

62

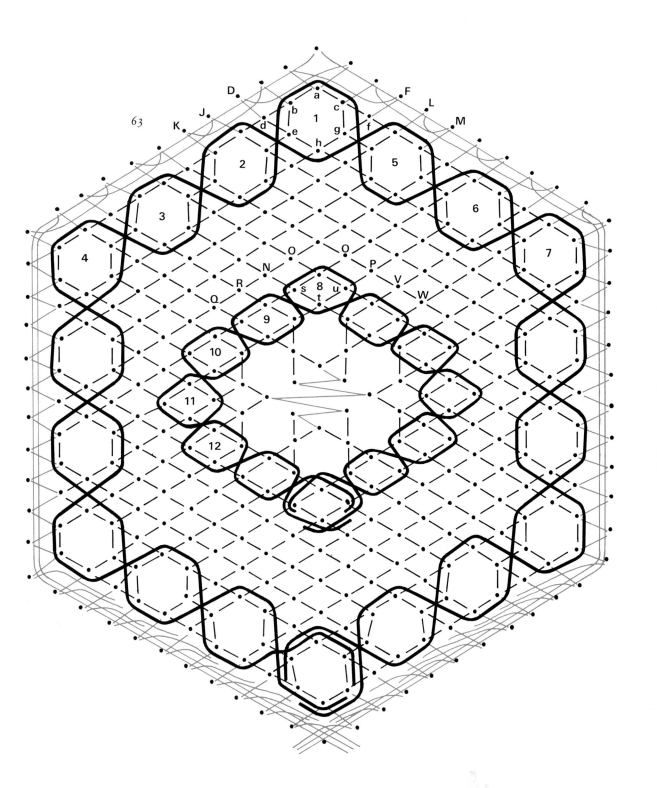

Pattern 18. Photograph 64.

Viewed from a distance it can be seen how careful stitch selection creates different effects, the cloth diamonds assume little importance and the circular patterns are accentuated. It is suggested that the lacemaker selects two 'fillings' to make an attractive length and pricks her requirements using pricking 65. Refer to diagram 66.

Working information

1. In the honeycomb there is no centre hole at the bottom and pairs are taken through for the next feature. Similarly the top hole is missing and continuous rows are worked without a top link later in the pattern.
2. At the side point of the cloth diamond the weaver travels out round the gimp, is twisted and travels on through the passive pairs to make a picot and then returns to complete the weaving.
3. The hole in the centre of cloth is explained on page 42.
4. Tallies are worked in place of ground stitches and the same pairs used.

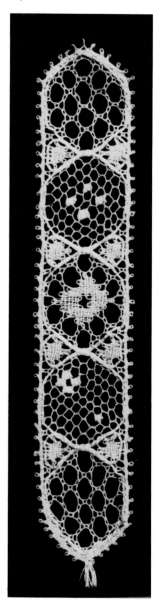

64

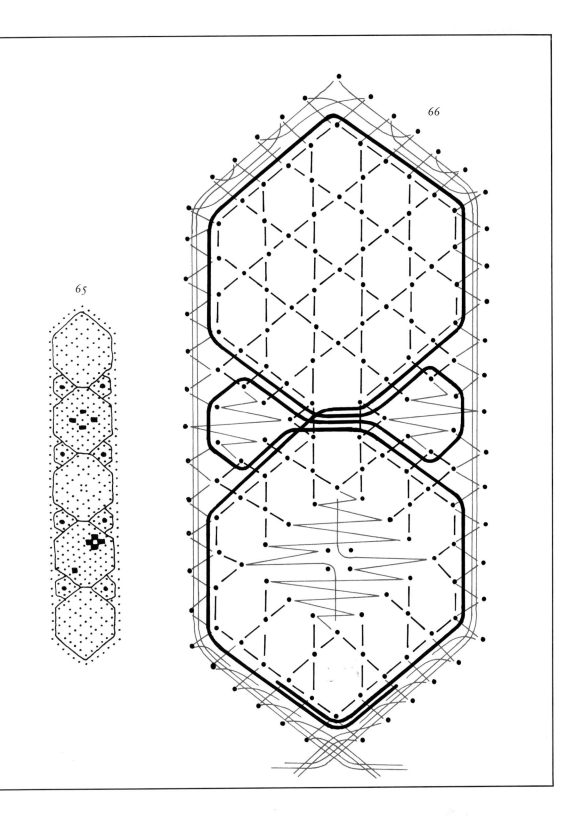

65

66

Pattern 19. Photograph 67.

Any hexagon or sampler with pointed ends can be worked with a footside edge.

Two pairs extra are required, one for each footside edge. Insertions require two straight edges and any straight sided sampler may be worked as a length. Prepare pricking 68 and refer to diagram 69.

Unlike previous patterns, pairs are not introduced from the outside rows of holes.

Hang four pairs on pin A, so that the outer threads are from the same pair and the inner threads from the same pair. Twist the two left-hand threads three times, twist the two threads immediately to the left of pin A three times.

Work cloth stitch and three twists with the threads to the right of pin A.

The outside pairs become the footside edge pairs, one in each direction and the inner pairs the weavers.

Hang four pairs as before on a support pin at Z. Weave the pair to the left of A through the four threads falling to the right of Z. Weave the pair from the right of A through the same four threads. Incline these threads across the pillow, put up pin 6 below these passive threads, between the pairs from A and cover with cloth stitch. The right-hand pair works the footside sequence to C and back to d. Remove pin Z. Replace pin Z and hang up one pair to be taken in with cloth stitch before pin d is placed in position. The weaver (fourth pair) works the footside sequence again and pin E is used. Continue, adding one pair at e and f and two pairs at g. Note that one pin has no connection with the ground or honeycomb but facilitates the movement around the bend. Pin h is a catch pin put in position to the right of both pairs when the ground stitch is worked.

The left side is worked similarly. The left-hand pair from b works the footside sequence out to the left. Work two cloth stitches through the passive pairs.

Twist the weaver three times. Work cloth stitch and three twists with the outside edge pair, place the pin to the right of both pairs, ignore the outer pair and bring the inner pair back through the two passive pairs. Pin Y may be used as a support pin when introducing pairs. At catch pin n the pin is placed to the left of both pairs. Remember that the catch pin always lies adjacent to the passive pairs.

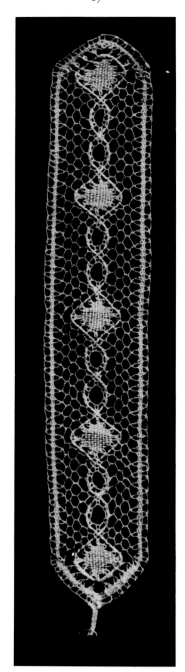

67

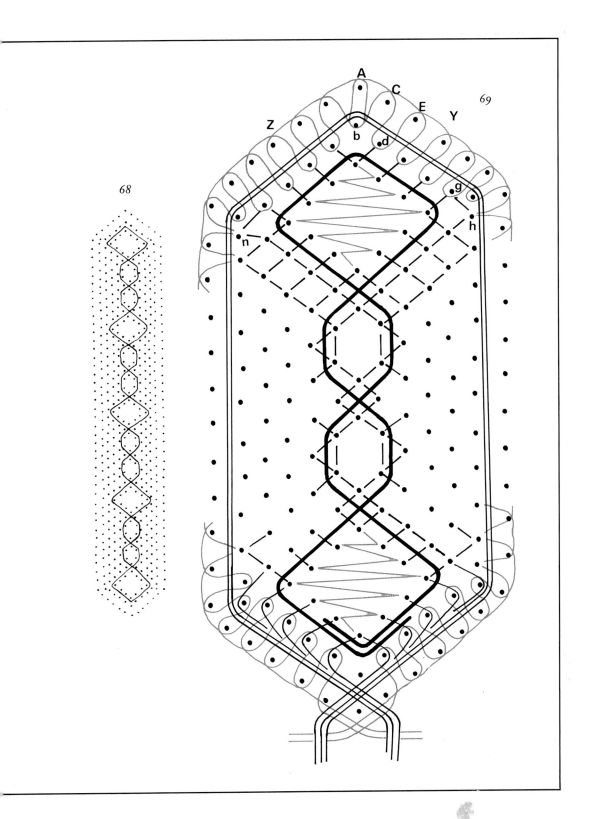

Pattern 20. Photograph 70.

All the techniques used in this piece have been used in previous patterns.
Prepare pricking 71 and refer to diagram 72.
For additional help refer to these pages:
Introducing picots   page 52.
Working the headside   page 22.
Cloth diamond   page 61.
Hole in cloth   page 42.
Cloth diamond with weaver making picot   page 58.
Ending   page 51.

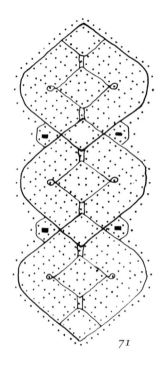

71

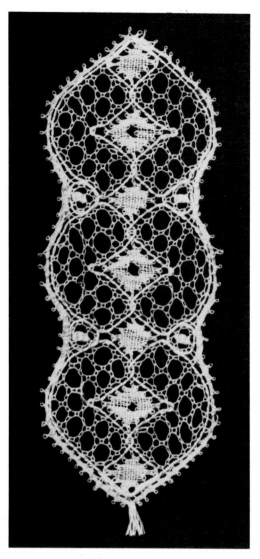

70

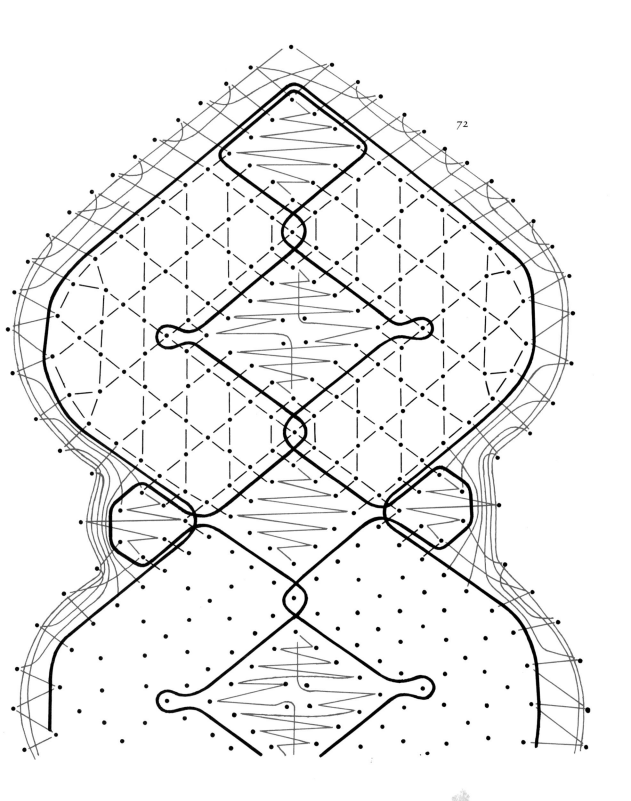

72

Pattern 21. Photograph 73.

Prepare pricking 74 and refer to diagram 75. With knowledge gained from previous patterns and close reference to the diagram this attractive piece of lace is very straightforward to make.

Additional advice: Work the continuous honeycomb row from a to b and the gap row from c to d. Remember to make a picot before working pin d. A pair from the diamond and a pair from c work cloth stitch, pin e, cloth stitch. The right-hand pair is weaver and weaves to k. Pairs are brought in on the left at pin g as far as pin j and left out from f as far as k. Work the other side.

Work the honeycomb diamonds with a tally in the centre of each and ensure that one gimp thread is used to enclose both diamonds, thus avoiding a hole in the middle.

Taking particular care on the headside continue to weave the cloth trail.

Complete the honeycomb.

Picots are worked normally. When the last pair, from p, has worked the picot it travels back through five passive pairs, two permanent passives and three pairs required for picots. Picots from Q to R should be worked as a single operation.

74

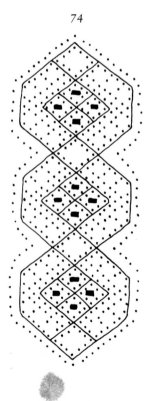

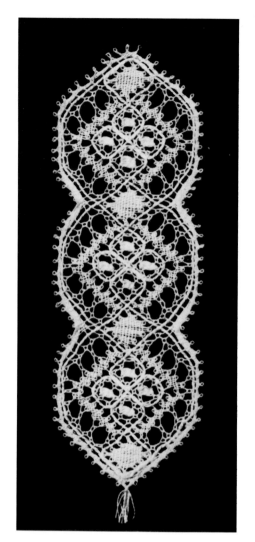

73

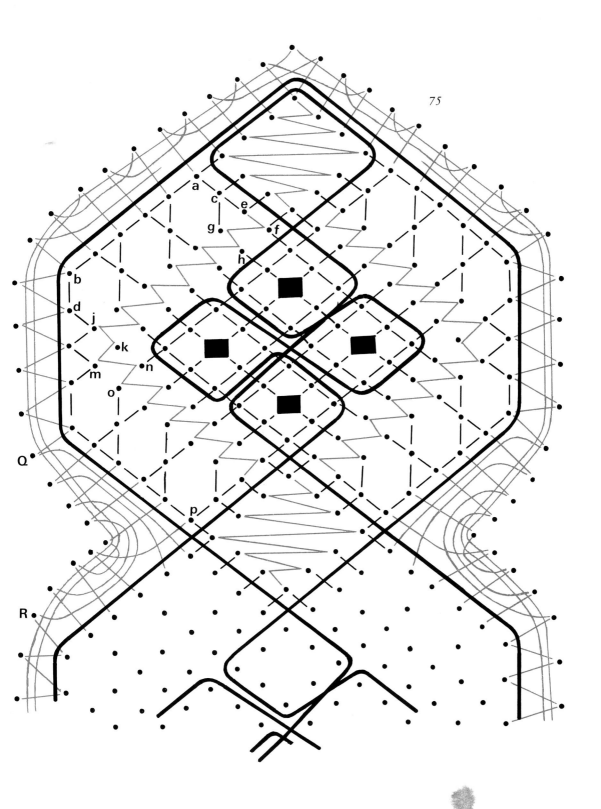

five
Circular & Motifs

These can be worked quickly and easily with few
bobbins using a six section pattern.

Pattern 22. Photograph 76.

Prepare twenty pairs of bobbins, one pair and one
single gimp thread and pricking 77.
Refer to diagram 78, also to pattern 11.
Position O is the centre of the motif. Place the
pricking in the centre of the pillow, use four cloths
to cover the edges. Ascertain that the top of the
pricking and the top of the diagram are in the same
position.
Picots: These must be worked from the beginning
of the pattern. Hang two pairs on A and make a
false picot. Hang six passive pairs on a support pin
at Z and bring both pairs from A through all
passive pairs. Make a false picot at B and bring the
right-hand pair through all six passive pairs. The
left-hand pair and the outside passive pair make a
cloth stitch, the third pair from the edge works to
the edge, makes a picot and travels back through
six pairs. Again the third pair goes out for picot D
and back through five pairs. Continue to G, two
passive pairs remain.
Honeycomb: Place the gimp threads as shown in
the diagram. Study the pattern and begin at pin a.
Work rings 1, 2 and 3, if necessary refer to pattern
15. If desired tallies can be placed inside each ring.
Arrows indicate the introduction of pairs over the
gimp thread. Work the continuous honeycomb
row from c to f. Take the right-hand pair from f
round the gimp to work honeycomb pin g with
another pair from a support pin. Bring left-hand
pair from g back round the gimp to work pin h.

76

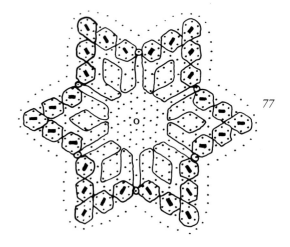

77

66

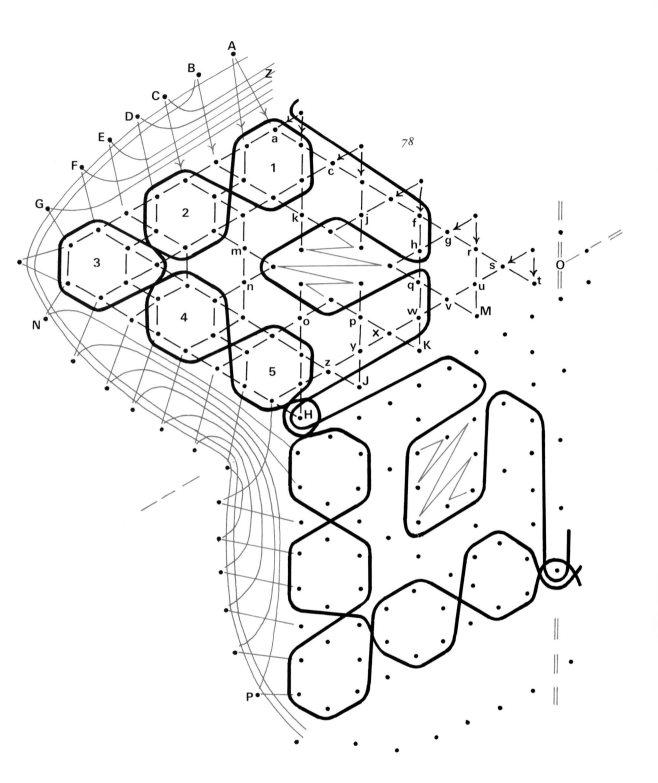

Work gap row pins j, k and m.

Take the gimp through six pairs to work the cloth diamond. Work honeycomb gap row pins n, o and p.

From g complete the diagonal row towards O introducing new pairs for pins r, s and t. Work honeycomb stitches u and v.

Work honeycomb pins w, x and y. Complete rings 4 and 5, this will include the last honeycomb pin at z. One pattern is complete.

Honeycomb pins H, J, K and M are worked as shown and the picot sequence from N to P is normal.

Turn the pillow for the next head: To facilitate working the last two sections, press the picot pins and pins supporting gimp threads down until the heads are close to the card. Slide a piece of rigid clear plastic under the cover cloths to lie over the pin heads. The threads will move over the plastic easily but the lace can be seen underneath.

To complete the motif

1. Refer to the edging on page 49.

2. If the lace is to be mounted permanently the ends should be knotted as described previously and then with the aid of a sewing needle taken through the mounting fabric and trimmed to one inch (25mm). They can be secured permanently using any iron-on interfacing, refer to page 113.

3. The threads should be knotted as described previously but the bobbins are not cut off. Starting at the centre with two pairs make a tight plait (continuous half stitch). Include all the pairs hanging from the pins as follows:

Take the next pair through the four plait threads in cloth stitch.

Take the next pair through two pairs in cloth stitch and work stitch movements (page 9) ababa with the edge pair. Continue to add pairs and work ababa on the right-hand edge. Gradually throw out pairs from the thickening cloth. Eventually the remaining threads are threaded alongside a gimp thread or woven, using a needle into the headside passives. This method may appear thicker but it avoids a lot of oversewing and is useful for the larger mats.

Pattern 23. Photograph 79.

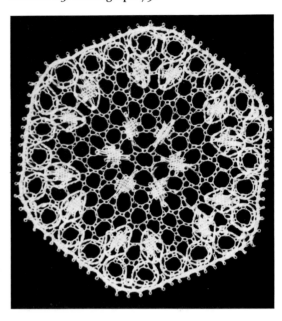

Prepare bobbins, one gimp pair and pricking 80. Refer to diagram 81.

This pattern is similar to pattern 8 but honeycomb is used instead of point ground.

The centre position is O.

Bring two pairs through a gimp to work pin A in honeycomb stitch.

Make a false picot at B. Hang one pair on a support pin at Z and bring the right-hand pair from B through the passive from Z and the left-hand pair from A. Take it round the gimp thread into ring 1. Work the edge pairs in cloth stitch and use the third from the edge for picot C, take it back into ring 1. Work the ring, taking pairs to the right for honeycomb and to the left for a picot. Cross the gimp threads and continue with the right-hand thread through six pairs, two from the ring, one from honeycomb and three from support pins. Work the cloth diamond, and the honeycomb and mayflower as far as possible, include pin a.

Work rings 2 and 3, another diamond and ring 4. The section is complete. Work honeycomb pins E, F, G, H, J and K as in the diagram, also picots b and c. (They correspond with B and C and provide pairs for the first ring in the next section.)

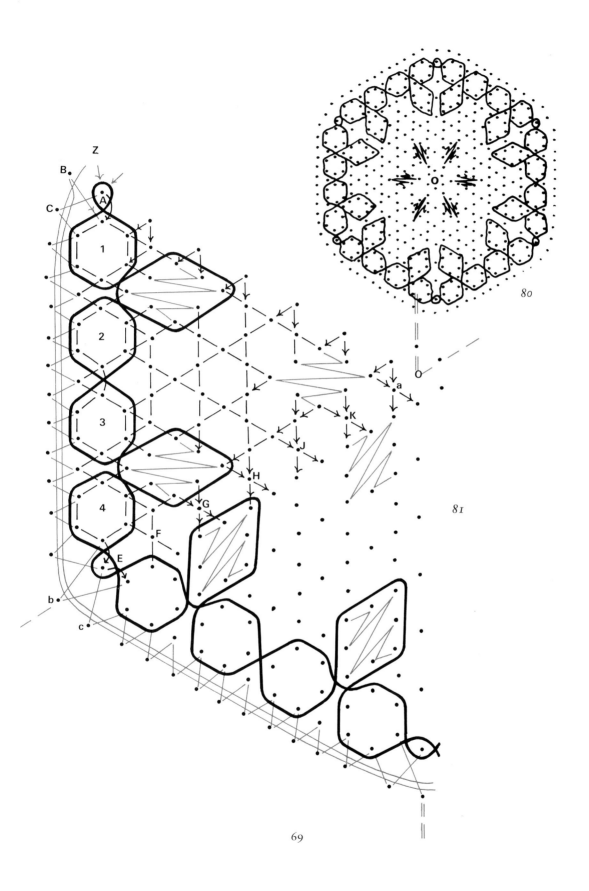

80

81

Pattern 24. Photograph 82.

Prepare bobbins, one pair and one single gimp thread and pricking 83.

Refer to diagram 84.

Make a false picot at A and take it through five passive pairs on a support pin at Z. The remaining four picots are made using the third passive pair from the edge as usual.

Honeycomb pin B is enclosed with a gimp pair.

Work buds 1 and 2, honeycomb pin a and picot b.

Work the top and left-hand side of bud 3 and then picot c.

Work the cloth diamond taking the weaver round both gimp threads to work the side honeycomb pin in bud 3. This will appear neater if cloth stitch and two twists is used instead of the normal honeycomb stitch.

Complete the diamond, bud 3 and honeycomb pin d. Work buds 4 and 5.

Work the picots from D to E and note that the picot pair at e returns immediately into the next bud.

The section is complete. Work honeycomb gap row pins F, G and H and the gimp enclosed pin. *Turn the pillow.* Work five more sections.

This pattern can be worked without a gimp outlining the cloth diamond.

82

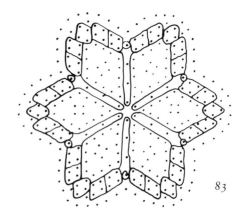

83

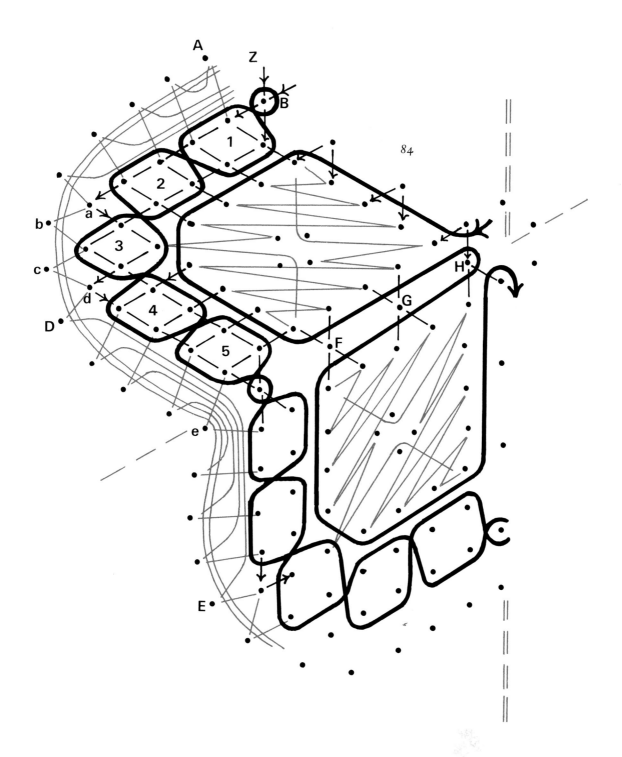

84

six
fillings

In most traditional patterns honeycomb is the popular 'filling'. It is attractive and compact and looks well in any space however small. In larger areas tallies or mayflowers can be added to create a variety of effects. Many of the other 'fillings' are found only in wide floral patterns where the spaces to be filled are large and irregular. As stitches in a hexagonal area much of their beauty is lost, but nevertheless they provide interesting alternatives and are easier to master in a geometric situation.

Pattern 25. Sampler. Photograph 85.

Prepare bobbins, two pairs of gimps and pricking 86.

To begin: Refer to diagram 87A. Set in false picots and introduce the gimp thread.

Work honeycomb pins in both directions from a to b and c. Introduce the second gimp thread and twist pairs twice for honeycomb. Remember that pairs travel out from b to make a picot on the left at d and to the right for honeycomb pin e. Returning round the gimp thread they are ready for pin f. Note that catch pins are used to improve the appearance of the ground.

A. Old mayflower

Refer to diagram 87A. This is a variation of honeycomb and mayflower used in earlier patterns. Each cloth diamond has four holes on each side instead of three. To work the diamond make a cloth stitch at g and proceed to pins h and j as usual. At k and m there are no pairs to add. Twist the weaver and continue to n and o where pairs enter the cloth. After pins n and o pairs will be left out, after p and q nothing is left out and the remaining pairs complete the diamond at r, s and t. When pins are removed there are loops at k and m and p and q; on a fine pattern this looks very attractive but may appear untidy if the pattern is coarse and thread thick.

B. Vertical bars of cloth with tallies

Refer to diagram 87B. It is important to select the correct pair as weaver for each trail. It will look neater if the weaver travels through the trail pairs before the first pin is put in position. Similarly it should work back through the trail pairs after the last pin has been placed. Tallies are made with the weavers and it is necessary to mark the pricking accurately, the tally is worked at the third pin hole.

C. Lattice (Four pin cloth blocks)

Refer to diagram 87C. Follow the diagram carefully noting that the weavers remain the same throughout. The weaver always travels across the top of the block and the pin holes are worked abcd. After pin d the weaver travels to the right through the three pairs in the block and on through two pairs more before pin A is put in position. The weaver travels back through three pairs to B and then to C and D.

D. Alternate honeycomb

Refer to diagram 87D. The gap row pins are arranged differently from the usual form of honey-

85

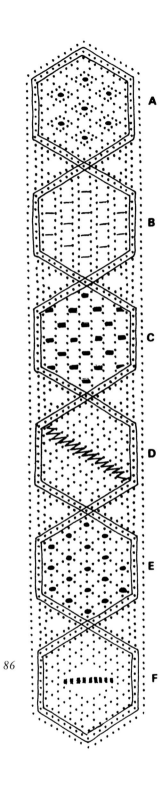

A

B

C

D

E

86

F

73

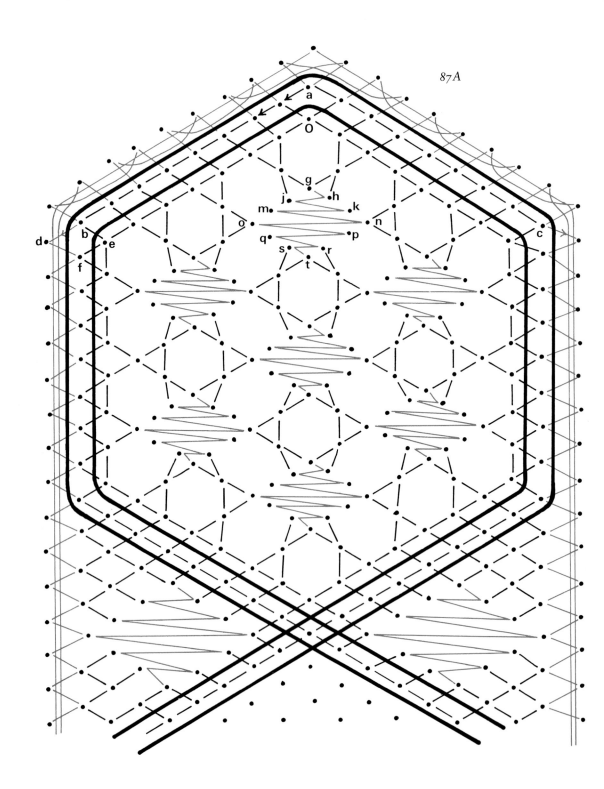

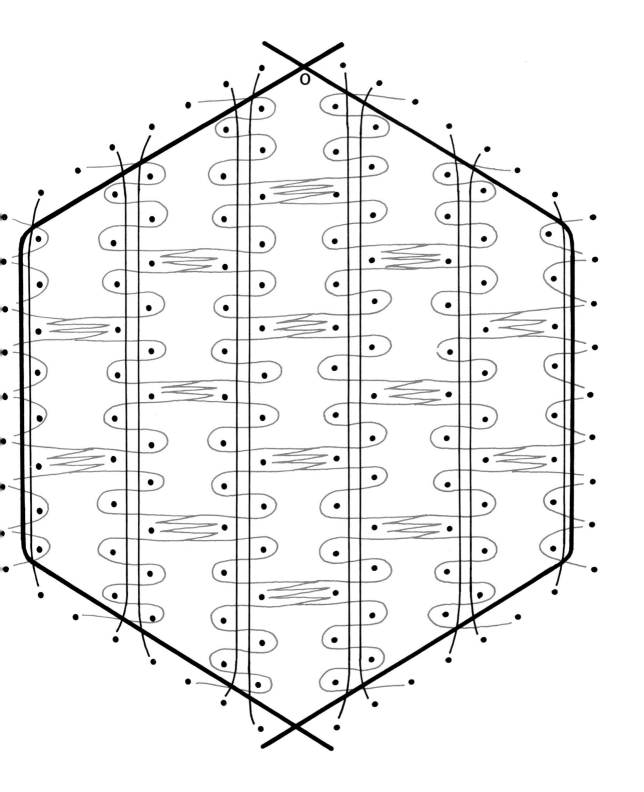

O

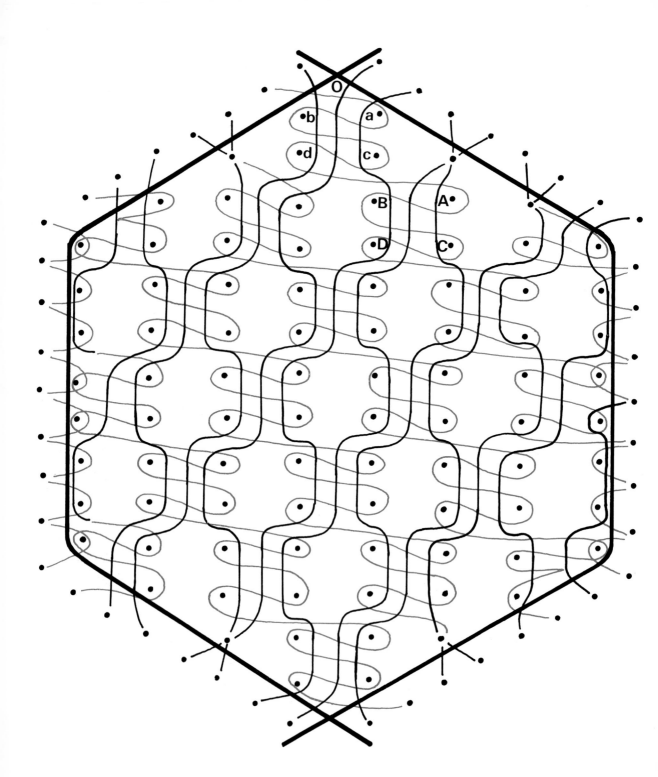

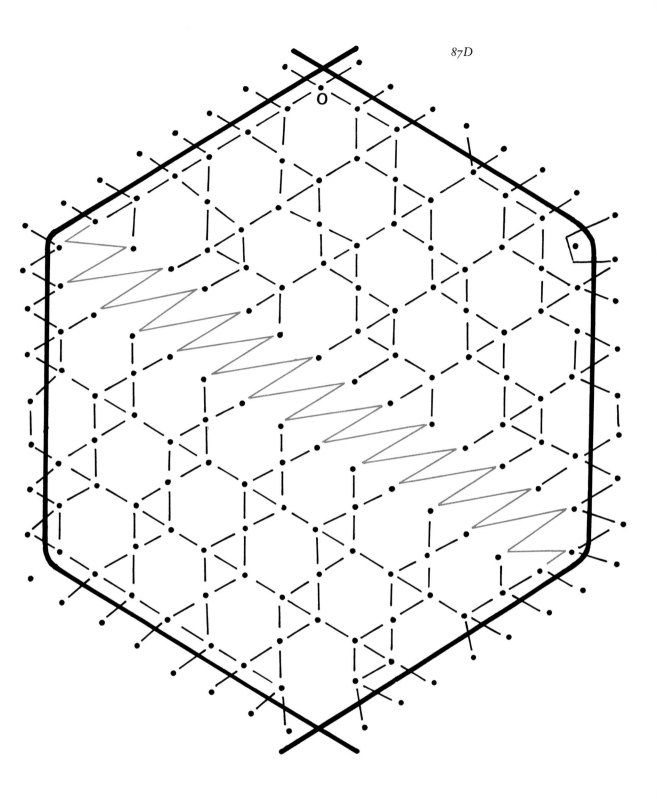

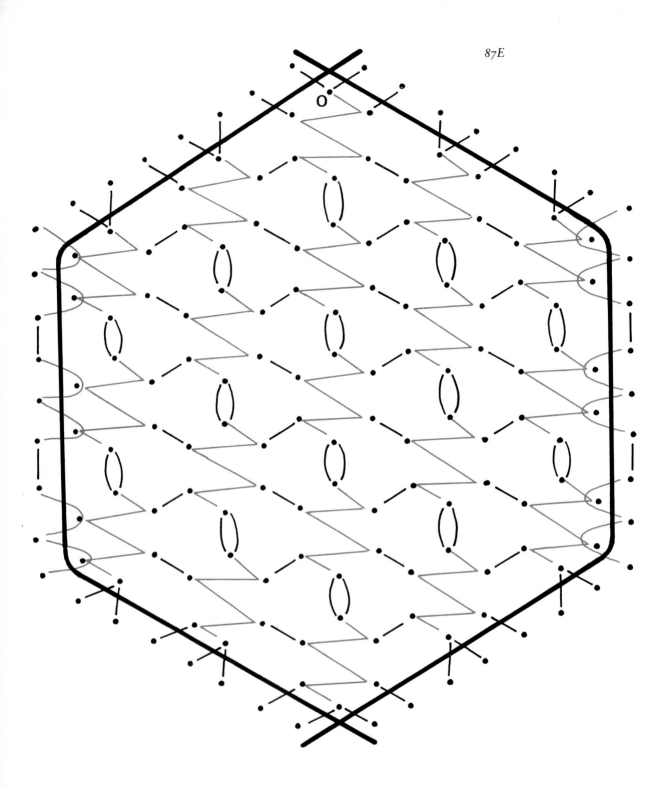

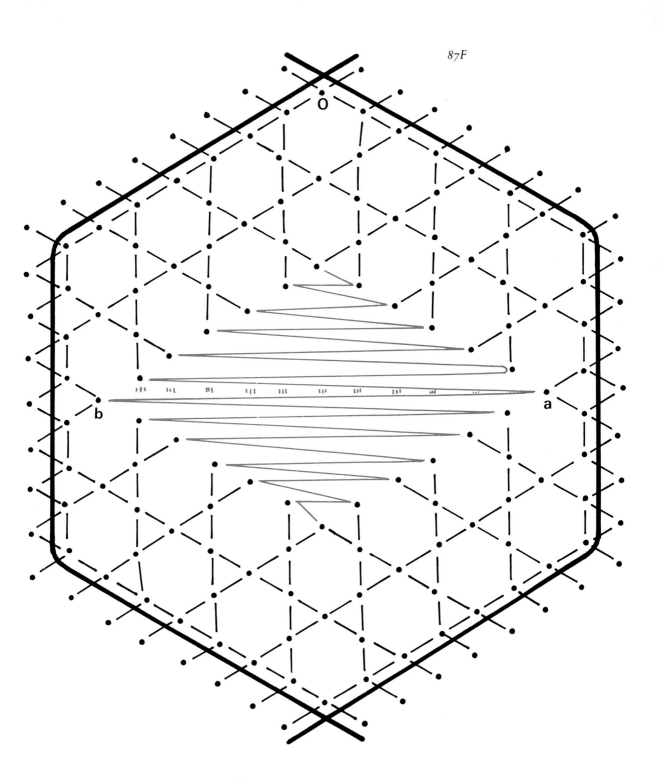

comb and there are no vertical pairs. It is interesting to observe that the bold lines on the lace are not
the continuous rows on the pricking.

E. Another cloth filling – old name unknown

Refer to diagram 87E. Today this is sometimes
known as the star filling as the clothwork appears
to have six points. Pairs which leave the side pins
are twisted twice and the bottom pin is covered
with cloth stitch and twist. Before the pin is put in
at the top of the clothwork the same pairs receive a
cloth stitch. This makes a short plait and separates
the clothwork.

F. Honeycomb with cloth diamond

Refer to diagram 87F. No collection of fillings is
complete without honeycomb. In the centre of the
diamond, when pin a is in position all the passive
pairs are twisted once and then the weaver is taken
to b. This helps to maintain good tension and
vertical passive threads in a large area of cloth.
The sampler is completed as described on page 51.

Pattern 26. Circular mat. Photograph 88.

The fillings are identical with those in the sampler.
Pricking 89 may be copied or other fillings in the
sampler used instead. To use other fillings, prick
the mat leaving the hexagonal areas empty. Place
rigid clear plastic under the sampler and copy the
fillings required. Place these on the mat pricking
and prick the new filling onto the card. To ensure
that the top hole is in the correct position use O as a
guide.
To begin: Set false picots on a and b and seven pairs
on a support pin. Allow both pairs from each picot
to work through all seven pairs. Then take the
third pair out to make the next picot and bring it
back through six pairs.
Continue until all picots are made, and bringing
the picot pair through one less passive each time.
The pattern: Work the honeycomb pins between
the gimp threads and then the filling. Honeycomb
is worked towards the centre and the diamond
completes the section at the point. As usual there
are honeycomb gap row pins between the sections.
Instructions for working six section mats are given
on page 68.

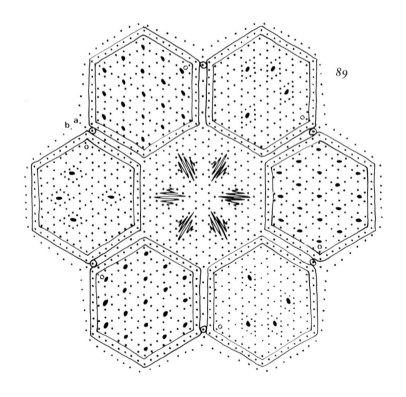

89

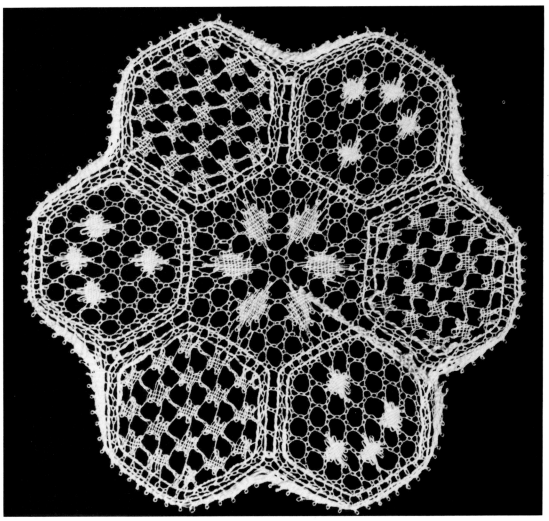

Pattern 27. Photograph 90.

This motif should be worked before the larger mat in photograph 93.

Prepare bobbins, one pair of gimp threads and pricking 91.

Refer to diagram 92.

This appears more complicated as there is no gap stitch row to separate the sections.

To begin: Work section A. Hang three pairs on the left and ten on the right on support pins and pass a gimp pair through all thirteen pairs. Work the cloth feature and bring the gimps together for section C.

To introduce pairs on the picot edge: This is section B, make a false picot at b and take the right-hand pair through five passive pairs hung on a support pin.

Work four more picots in the usual way.

Work section C as far as c. The weaver is taken to the edge to make picots in this pattern.

Work honeycomb section D as far as possible.

Work cloth and picots in section E to provide the pairs to complete the honeycomb in section F.

Complete the cloth in section G, cross the gimp threads.

Picots are worked as usual in section H.

Follow the arrows on the diagram carefully to work section J. Honeycomb pins are worked at e, f and g.

Turn the pillow. The pairs are ready to work section A again.

At k there is one extra pair to be dropped out and taken alongside the gimp thread to join the headside passives. Eventually it is used for a picot.

90

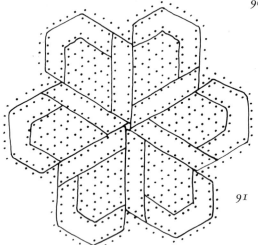

91

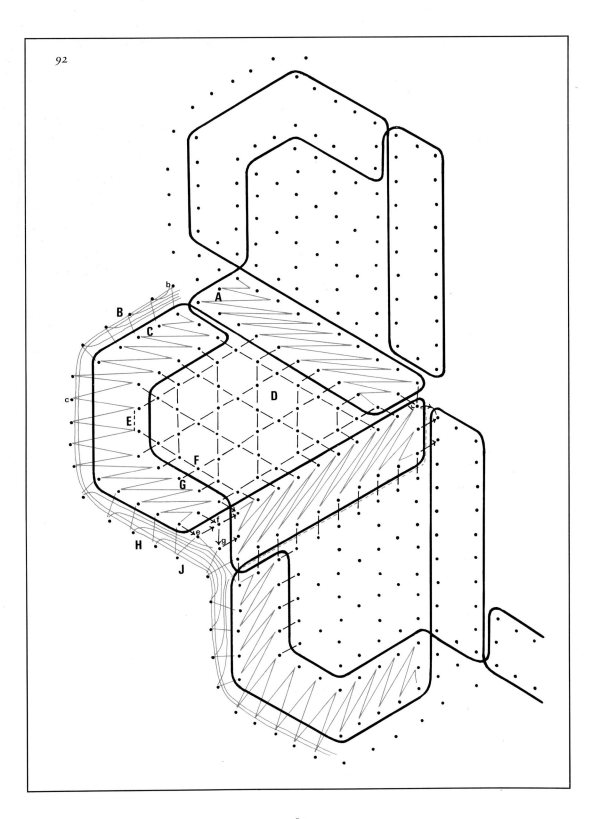

92

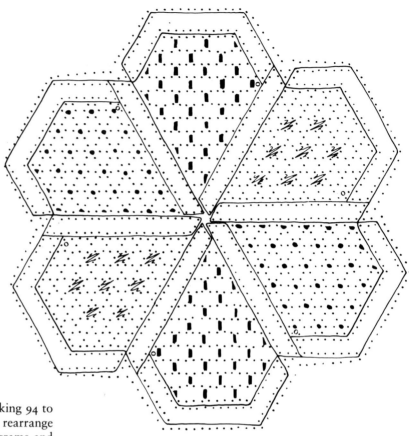

Pattern 28. Photograph 93.

The lacemaker may choose to use pricking 94 to match the photograph or select and rearrange fillings as desired. Pattern 25 gives diagrams and instructions for working the fillings. It is recommended that the lacemaker works the sampler for practice. The cloth features and the headside are similar to the previous pattern and a clear understanding of the smaller motif would assist the lacemaker here.

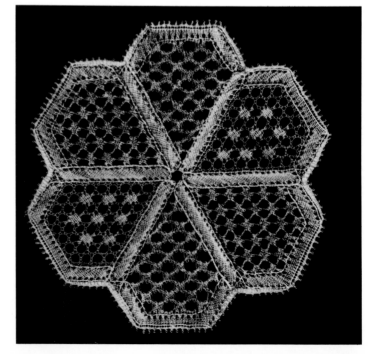

Author's Comment

Twenty-seven graded patterns provide the lacemaker with a good basic knowledge of Bucks Point lace. The basic techniques should be understood and the need for a logical approach appreciated. There are so many traditional patterns, a visit to Luton Museum or any other collection to see pattern drafts and dealers' sample books should convince any enthusiast that it is essential to be able to work without diagrams and written instructions. The aim of the lacemaker should be to 'read' the pricking, and from that interpretation, make the lace. This coveted ability comes only with experience and a willingness to try.

The basic techniques cannot be changed. They serve to produce a lace that is attractive and durable with the features that are traditional and desirable to make lace recognised as Bucks Point. For example, two passive cloth stitch pairs and a straight footside edge, the catch pin and ground stitches with three twists; the covered honeycomb pins with a definite order for working to achieve threads travelling in three directions are all characteristic of this lace. Firm double picots and a minimum of two passive pairs on the headside, the use of fine thread and a closely pricked pattern and features outlined with a soft loosely woven gimp soon become familiar and it would be unthinkable to alter them.

However the lacemaker will realise that some rules learned when working the regular patterns can, with caution and common sense, be broken as skills develop and more elaborate patterns are attempted. For example, we learn that the weaver always stays inside the gimp threads and passive pairs move out diagonally and return. And yet, in pattern 20 the weaver travelled to the edge to make a picot and there were no twists between cloth diamond and gimp thread. A glance at the pattern and the reason is obvious. In patterns with flowers, twists between gimps will separate and enhance the petals. However, when two threads lie together in a geometric pattern they often look better merging as one. False picots provide pairs to start a pattern. The aim when beginning a new pattern is to provide an edge in keeping with the normal headside. The precise use of pairs and false picots is unimportant, two lacemakers using common sense, initiative and a feeling for the lace will work differently and both produce an acceptable result. Only close scrutiny will reveal the differences, both are equally correct. When possible the normal headside sequence should be used as it uses the minimum of stitches to achieve a close and neat result.

Too many geometric patterns, too many patterns with diagrams and instructions can destroy the adventure that lies ahead. Avoid reliance on diagrams, recognise the fact that designs were created from flowers and leaves and the beauty lies in the natural lines and curves. Narrow laces imitate the floral shapes on a grid and delightful lace can be made, but the old patterns had the grid ground and honeycomb holes pricked in as required, and the floral design was added independently 'by eye'. The standard of the finished lace depended on the skill of the lacemaker who 'married' together the freedom of the design with the ground in which it is set. Eventually it becomes impossible to put instructions for a wide floral pattern on paper, the skilled person uses her knowledge adapting it when necessary.

To reassure those people who are not yet ready for this adventure, many of the patterns in the last section have diagrams and most are regular. Full written instructions are not given, but advice and references. Every pattern uses traditional methods, but no pattern is old; each has been designed with today's requirements in mind.

Note: When on the pillow the right side of the lace is nearest the card. Therefore certain patterns in the last section will appear as a reversal of the pricking in the photograph as they have been mounted.

seven
Twenty-seven Original Designs

This is a collection of patterns created especially for the lacemaker who wants something different but has only a limited time to give to the craft. Each can be mounted for a specific purpose. Any pricking can be enlarged or reduced on a modern photocopier and slight alteration may make it suitable for a particular use. However it would be unwise to work with less than twelve holes to the inch (25mm) on a vertical row of ground pins. Similarly a pricking with more than sixteen holes to the inch (25mm) presents difficulties as it is almost impossible to find suitable threads.

Four Designs for Brooches or Pendants. Patterns 28–31. Photograph 95.

Prickings and diagrams share the same numbers. Diagrams explain the working method. In diagram 96B, the first six pin honeycomb ring, the side pairs remain within the ring and make the second stitch. Working is as follows: Honeycomb stitch, pin b, honeycomb stitch, pin c, honeycomb stitch. The pair travels to pin d and d, e is worked as b, c. This avoids adding a new gimp pair. Rings in diagram 97B are worked similarly.

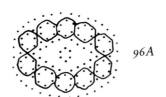

96A

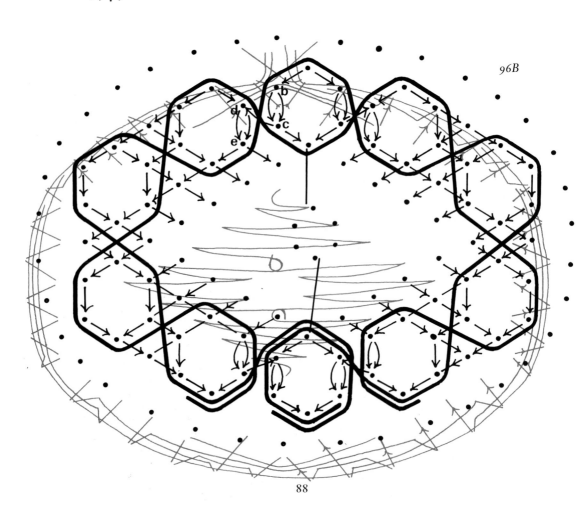

96B

88

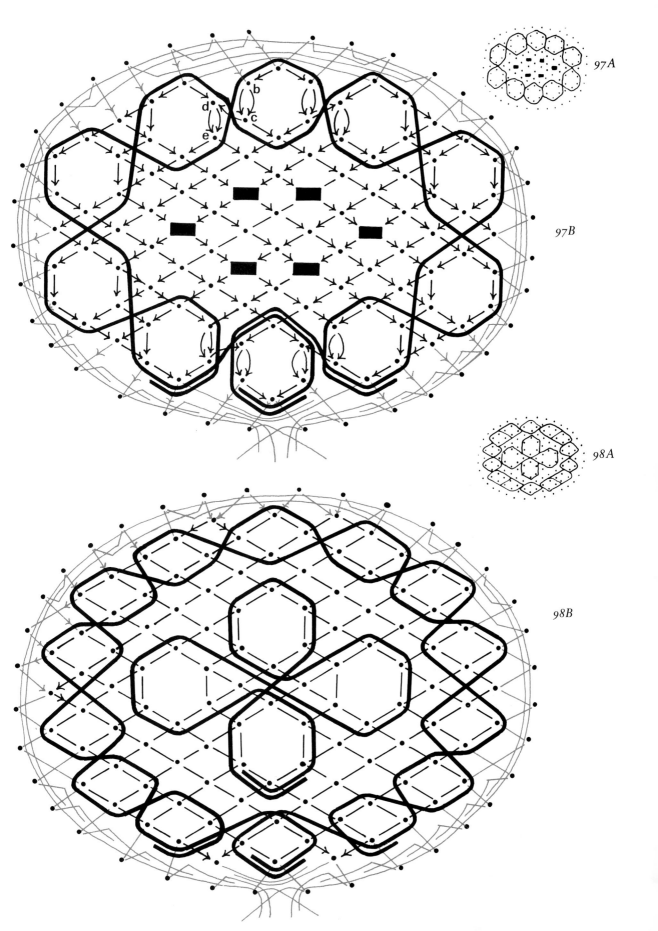

97A

97B

98A

98B

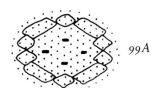

99A

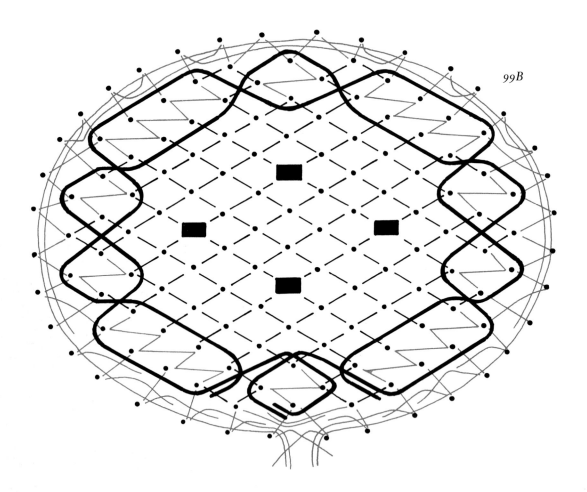

99B

Six Designs for Brooches, Pendants and Small Pill Boxes. Photograph 100.

Prickings and diagrams share the same numbers.

Pattern 32. 101A and B

Eight pairs of bobbins are required for this simple six section motif. Hang two pairs on pin a and cover with cloth stitch. The right-hand pair becomes the weaver and works through two more pairs in cloth stitch, pin b supports the weaver. One pair is added at each pin in the fan (d, f and h), and left out after pins on the other side. Note that the weaver is used for the honeycomb pin j; k and m are worked as indicated. A pair on a support pin works honeycomb pin m. The two outside passive pairs in the fan are plaited (continuous half stitch) and a picot made at n. They continue to form a plait as far as the next fan.

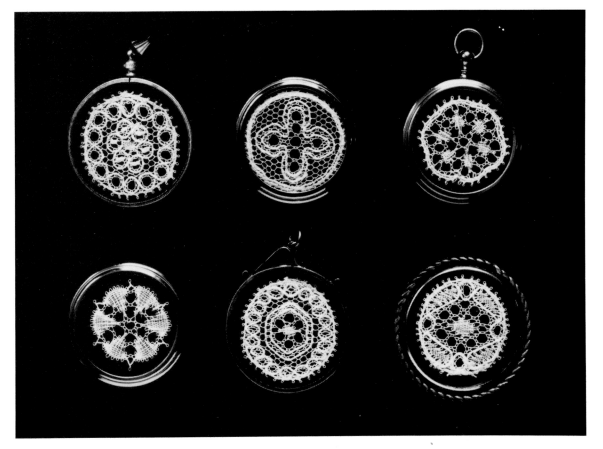

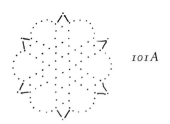

101A

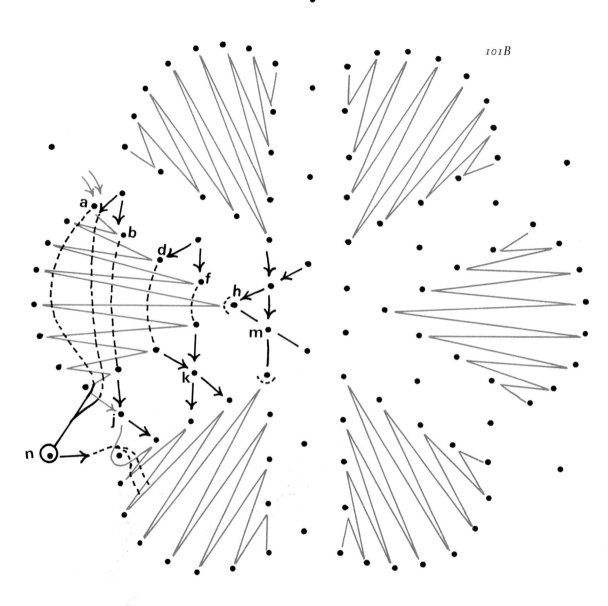

101B

Pattern 33. 102A and B

Ten pairs of bobbins and one gimp pair are
required. The ringed holes indicate support pin
positions when starting. On the headside a false
picot should be worked at a and the right-hand
pair will pass through two passive pairs for the first
honeycomb stitch. Picot W and honeycomb
stitches X Y and Z are worked at the end of the first
section. Continue.

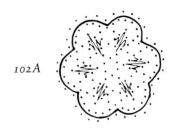

102A

102B

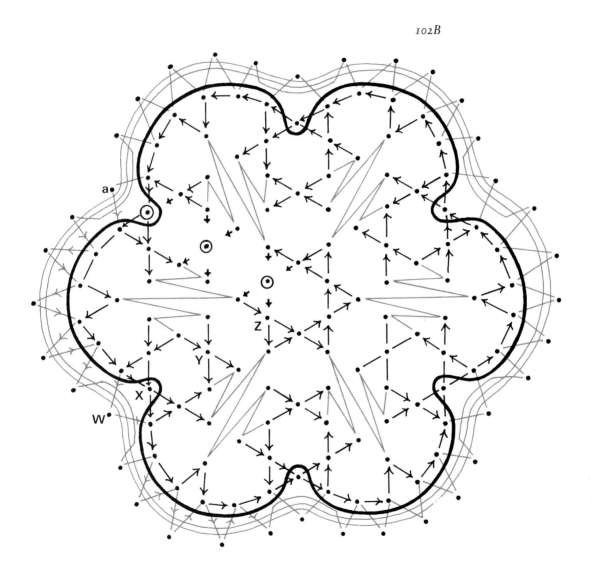

Pattern 34. 103A and B

The diagram explains the method, it is important
to pull the gimp threads which outline the honeycomb very firmly. Passive pairs are introduced
across the lace as in pattern 19.

103A

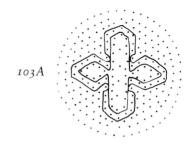

103B

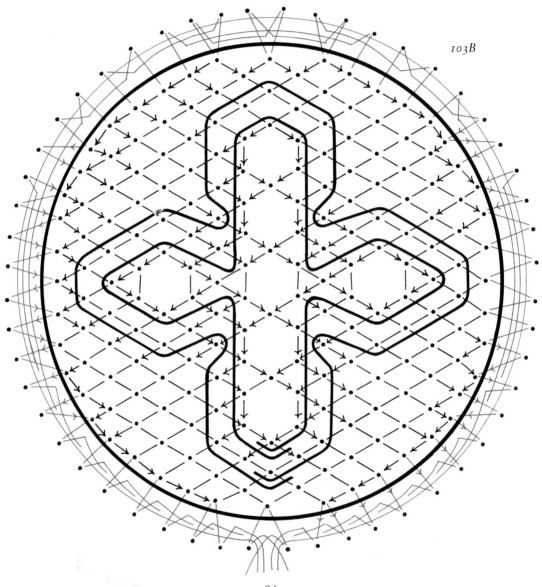

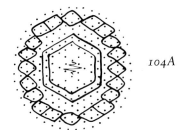

104A

Pattern 35. 104A and B

To create the impression of a circle six pairs are joined in across the lace to become three passives on either side. A similar method was used in pattern 19.

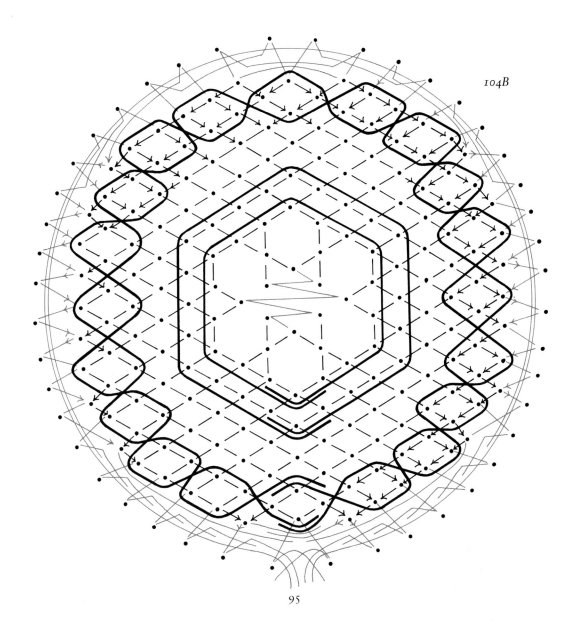

104B

Pattern 36. 105A and B

In some of the six pin honeycomb rings the method used in the oval brooch patterns, diagrams 96 and 97, is used. In the centre the small cloth diamond weaver travels into the rings to maintain a good shape.

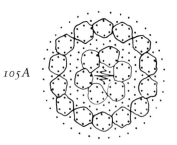

105A

105B

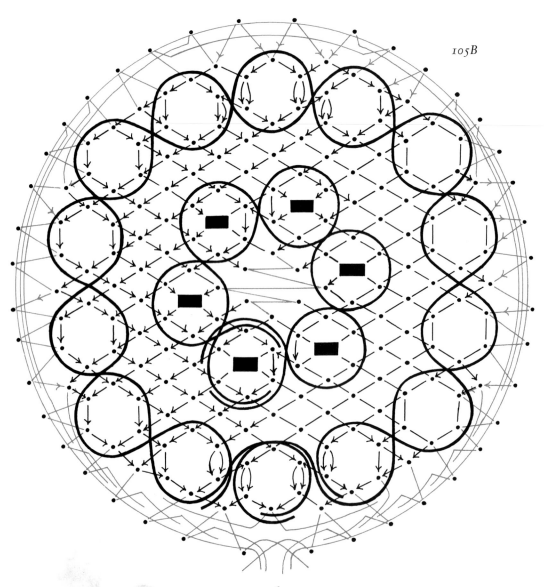

96

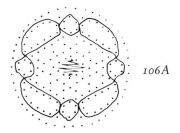

106A

Pattern 37. 106A and B

The top and bottom rings use the method described in diagram 96.

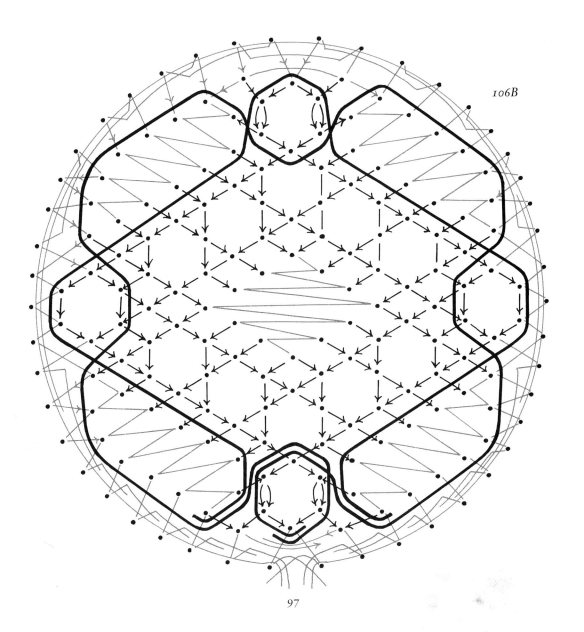

106B

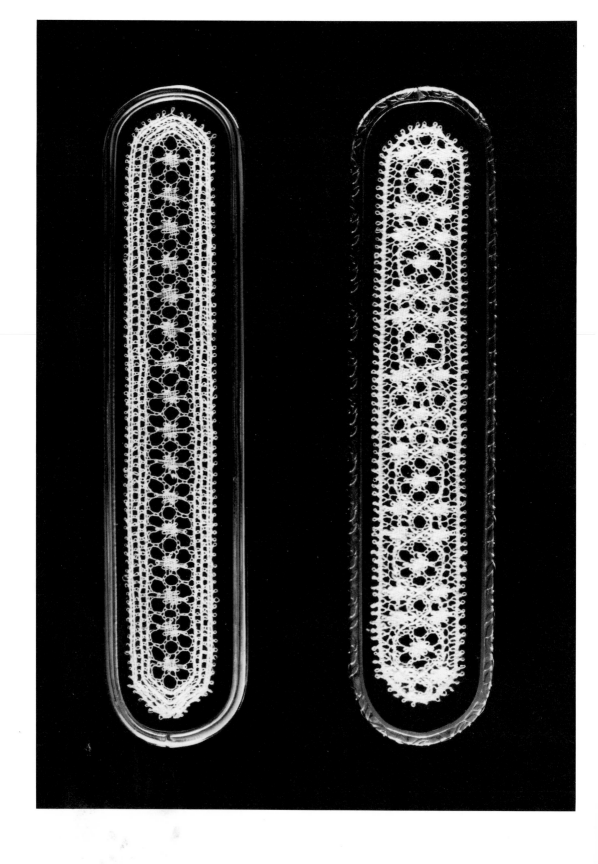

**Decorative Lace for Clothes Brushes. Patterns
38 and 39. Photograph 107. Pricking 108**

A. The lace is worked entirely with honeycomb
stitches, mayflowers and picots.
B. Catch pins are used on either side to maintain a
firm edge, it is important to pull the picot pair
tightly and tension the passive pairs.

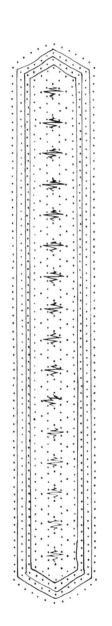

108

Circular and Oval Motifs

Pattern 40. Mounted in the top of a trinket box. Photograph 109.

Prepare pricking 110 and refer to diagram 111. Take two pairs from a support pin round a gimp thread and work honeycomb enclosed pin B. Make a false picot on A and take the right-hand pair through six passives supported behind the work. Work five normal picots to H. Hang two pairs on a support pin at C and pass the gimp through the necessary pairs before beginning the honeycomb. Work to abc. Take the gimp through pairs for pin d. Take the gimp back through four pairs.
Place pairs on support pins D, E and F and work the cloth diamond with a six pin hole.

To work the hole: Make the diamond in the usual way as far as g. When pin g is in position work back through three cloth pairs, put a pin between the weaver and last worked pair at h. Cover the pin with cloth stitch. Each pair becomes a weaver and weaves hjkmno and back to w or hrstuv and back to w. The weavers work a cloth stitch, put up pin w, cover the pin. One pair hangs as a passive and the other weaves to z.
Bring the gimp through five more pairs and complete the honeycomb.
Cross the gimp threads ready for the honeycomb pin. Work the gap row stitches and the picot head from J to K. Note that the picot pair from e travels back for the first honeycomb stitch in the next section.
Turn the pillow, work the next section.

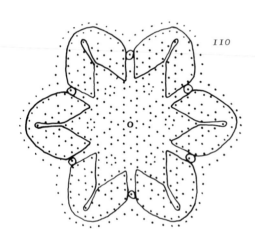

110

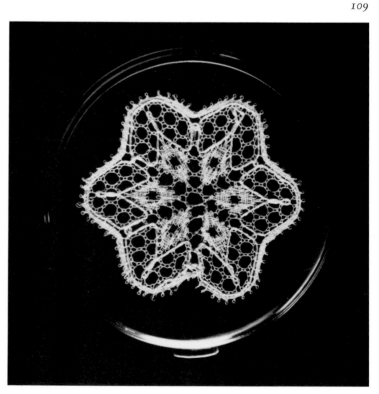

109

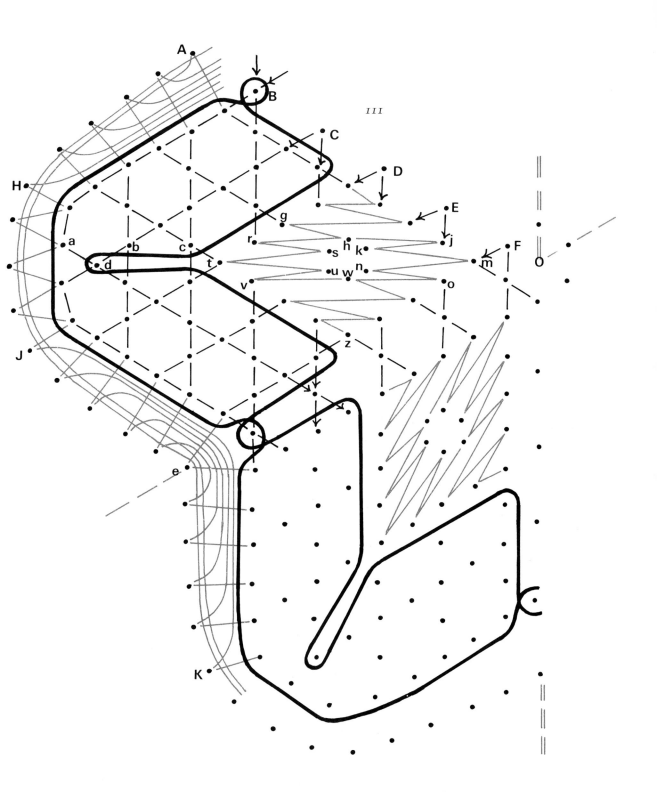

III

Pattern 41. Mounted in the top of a powder compact. Photograph 112.

Prepare pricking 113 and refer to diagram 114. This motif has six sections, alternating 'strawberry' and honeycomb. Refer to pattern 12.

To begin: Make a false picot on pin A and bring the right-hand pair through four passive pairs. Cloth stitch the outer pairs together before making a false picot on pin B. Bring the right-hand pair back through five passive pairs.

To work the cloth feature: Introduce five pairs from support pins round the gimp pair, also bring pairs from A and B round the gimp. Follow diagram 114, the left-hand passive travels out to work picot C and returns to the cloth, the right-hand passive at pin e travels out to the right to work the honeycomb stitch which begins the row to z. It returns for pin f and remains in the cloth for pin g. Cross the gimp threads below g.

To work honeycomb pin o: Work honeycomb pins j, k, m and n. Take the right-hand gimp thread through pairs from m, n and k. Work pin o.

To work the honeycomb and tally feature: Work honeycomb pin h and picots D, E and F. Take the gimp from o to the left through four honeycomb pairs, five cloth pairs and the pairs from pins h, D, E and F. Work the honeycomb feature and picot G. Complete the picot pins H, J and K and honeycomb pin p.

Work the second cloth feature including honeycomb pins q and r and picot M.

Picots N and O complete the section. Note that the left-hand pair from s make a picot and the right-hand pair hangs as inner passive pair. Turn the pillow.

To begin the second section work picots P, Q and R; picot S is worked at the same time as the second honeycomb ring. Work honeycomb pins t, u, v and w.

A new pair is introduced for pin w. The honeycomb ring begins with pin x.

Follow the diagram. Do not turn the pillow for the next section until the five honeycomb rings are completed at pin y.

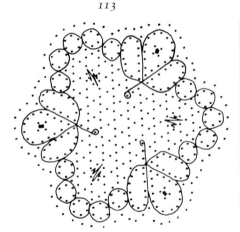

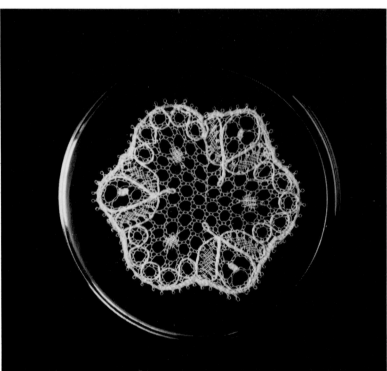

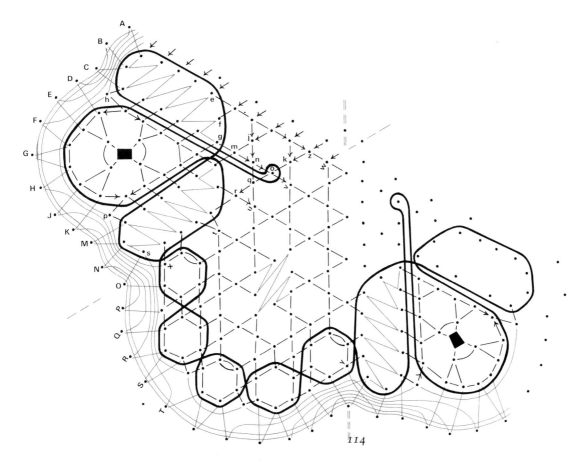

114

**Pattern 42. Mounted in a pendant frame.
Photograph 115.**

This piece of lace is worked using pricking 83 and
diagram 84. The single gimp thread is omitted.
Only the four pin buds are enclosed.

103

Pattern 43. Mounted in a key ring. Photograph 116.

Prepare pricking 117 and refer to diagram 118. This motif is worked from top to bottom. Pairs are introduced from picots, capital letters indicate false picots and small letters the normal picots. Hang four pairs on a support pin placed in the ringed dot above AB. To the left allow two pairs to hang from a false picot at A. Take the right-hand pair through the four threads hanging from the left of the support pin in cloth stitch. Similarly allow two pairs to hang from a false picot at B and bring the left-hand pair through the four threads to the right of the support pin in cloth stitch. The inner pairs from A and B lie together, cross them with cloth stitch. Work a false picot at C, ordinary picots at d and e and a false picot at F. On the other side work G, h, j and K. Begin honeycomb 1. Rings 2 and 3 must be worked at the same time as 1. Make picots m, N and o and p, Q and r as required. New gimps are required for rings 2 and 3. The gimp used for 1 is overlapped to surround 1 and then cut off. To work 4 and 5 picots s, T, u and V, and picots w, X, y and Z are required, note that there are three passive pairs on the headside, the extra pairs are needed for rings 6 and 7. For balance they are retained alongside 8 and 9. 10 is started with a new gimp pair and must be worked at the same time as 11 and 12. The method used to complete the motif has been discussed on page 51.

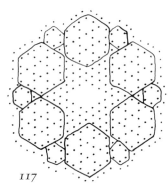

117

116

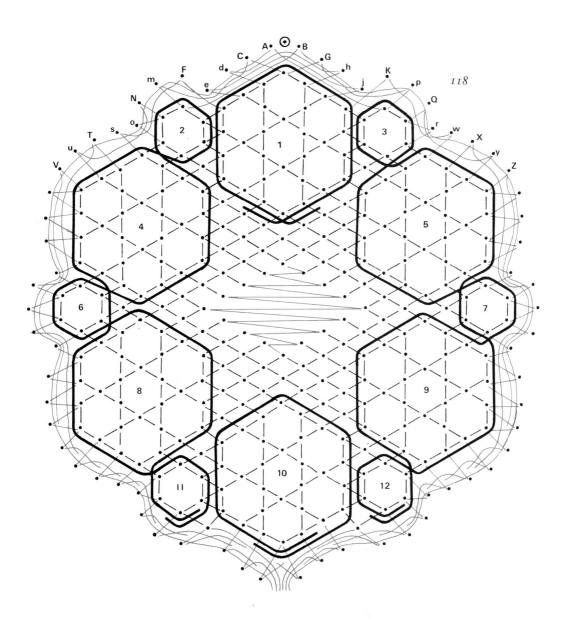

118

**Pattern 44. Mounted in an oval pendant.
Photograph 119.**

This pattern is an extended version of pattern 43.
Use pricking 120 and refer back to diagram 118.

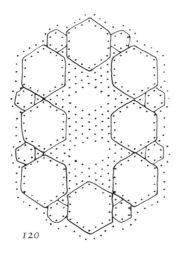

120

119

121

**Pattern 45. Mounted under a paperweight.
Photograph 121.**

Prepare pricking 122 and refer to diagram 123. Six
pairs of bobbins are introduced across the work to
provide three passive pairs in each direction. Pairs
are brought into the work from false and normal
picots alternately. All pins between the gimp and
picots are worked with honeycomb. All techniques
have been used in previous patterns. For a neater
result gimp threads may be placed through pairs
before working honeycomb pins a, b, c, d, e and f.

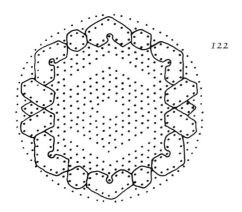

122

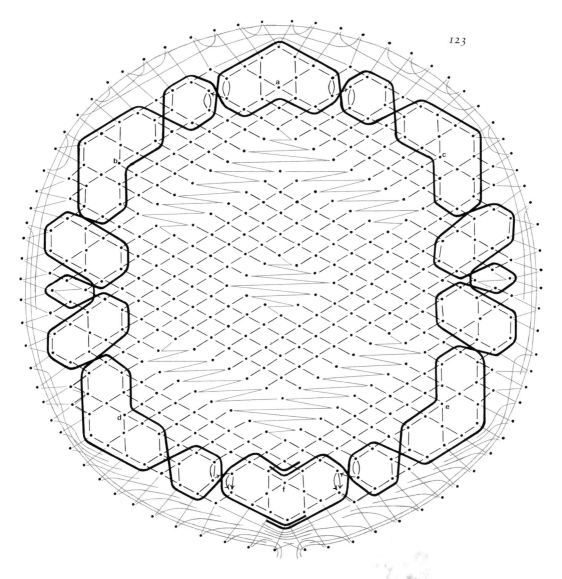

123

124

Pattern 46. Mounted in a circular pendant.
Photograph 124.

Prepare pricking 125 and refer to diagram 126. As
the pattern is symmetrical the picot arrangement
on the left-hand side can be worked with reference
to the right-hand side. If necessary, reference can
be made to pattern 15.

The flower centre is worked using three pairs of
gimp threads and the weaver in the cloth stitch
diamond passes untwisted round the gimp threads
for pin a and b.

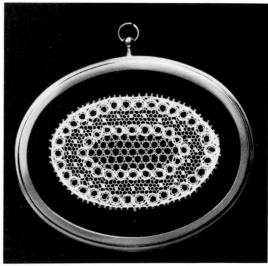

127

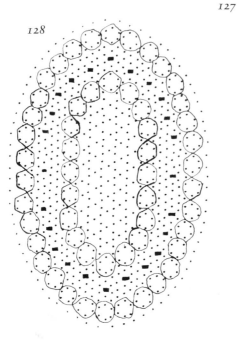

128

Pattern 47. Mounted in an oval frame.
Photograph 127.

There is similarity between pricking 128 required
for this motif and pricking 125. In pricking 128 the
honeycomb holes between gimp and picots are
omitted and cloth stitch and two twists is worked
instead of the honeycomb pin.

To achieve a neat headside, the inner passive pair is
sometimes used for the top hole in the honeycomb
ring, this occurs when there are insufficient picot
holes to provide all the pairs required. Refer to pin
a in diagram 131.

Refer also to b, c, d in the same diagram. Always
link the headside closely with the pattern feature
by taking a pair to make a picot and then returning
it to the pattern.

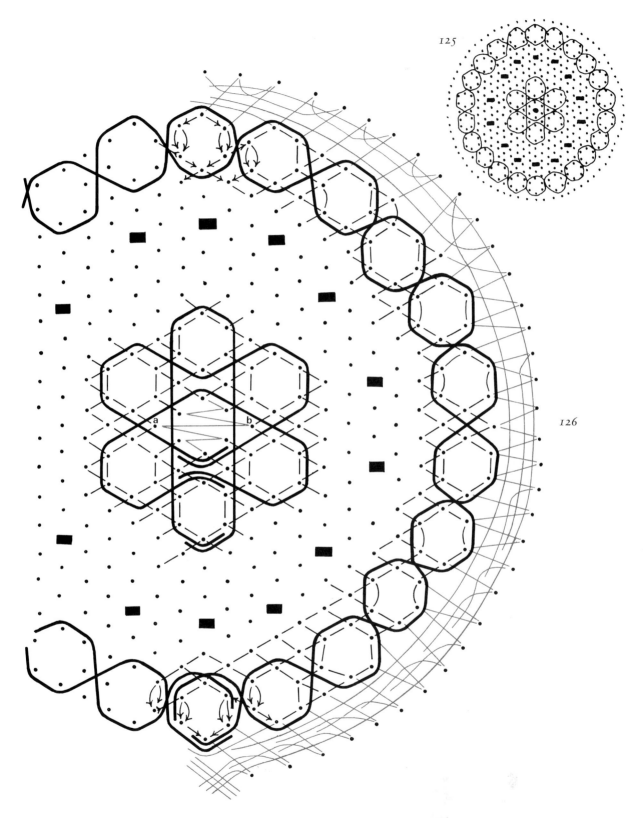

125

126

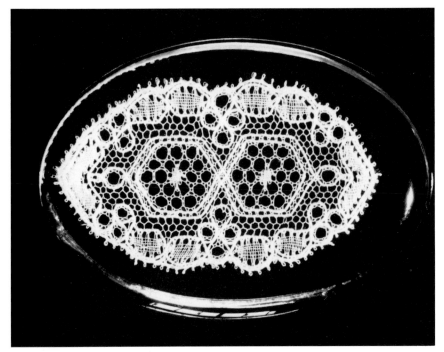

29

**Pattern 48. Mounted under a paperweight.
Photograph 129.**

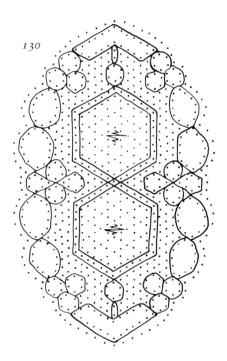

130

Prepare pricking 130 and refer to diagram 131.
This pattern is started in the same way as the
hexagons on pages 51 to 56. Note the addition of
two pairs of passive pairs in preparation for the
honeycomb rings. With experience the lacemaker
learns to anticipate the need for additional pairs
and the most attractive way of introducing them.
For example at false picot A both pairs enter the
work, also at pins a and o the inner passive pair is
used in the pattern feature. Rings 1, 2 and 3 are
worked numerically, and the right-hand side gimp
from ring 2 completely encircles ring 3 and then is
taken to the right-hand side of the cloth feature.
Also note the order of work for the four rings, and
that the left-hand gimp from ring 1 encircles rings 2
and 3 and the right-hand side of 4. This method
avoids unsightly holes. The lower half of the lace is
worked in the same way as the first half and the
pairs are discarded in the headside passive pairs as
in previous patterns.

110

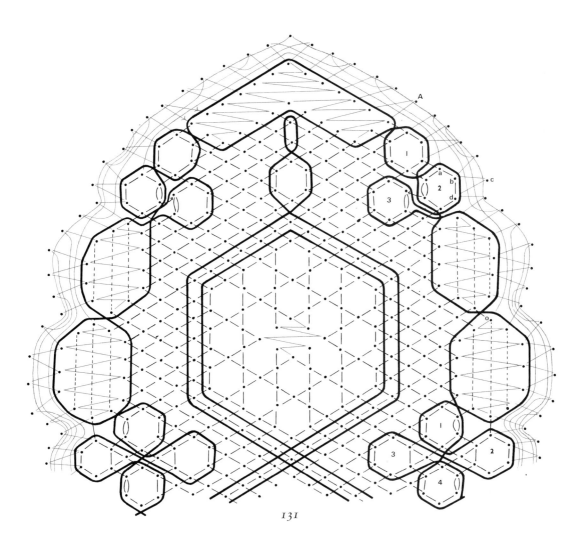

131

132

Pattern 49. Mounted in an oval frame.
Photograph 132.

Prepare pricking 133. The lace can be worked
following diagram 134 closely.

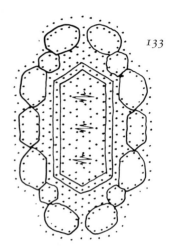

133

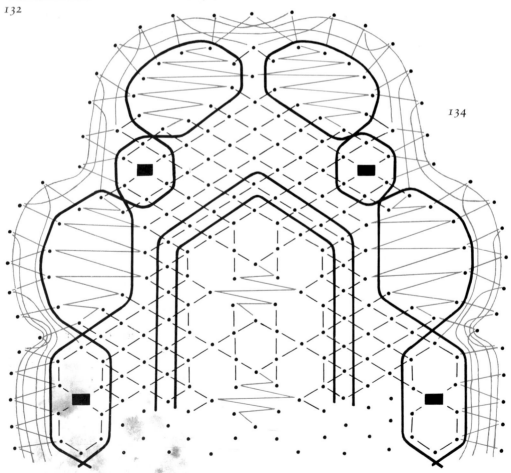

134

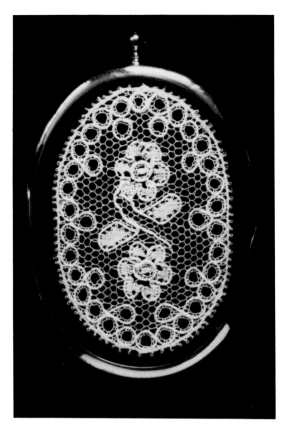

135

Pattern 50. Mounted in an oval frame. Photograph 135.

Prepare pricking 136 and work according to diagram 137. The only new technique is the use of gimp thread in the centre flower. Two pairs of gimp threads are required, one to encircle the petals and the other for the centre six pin ring.

To work the flower: Work the ground to supply pairs for the flower and put the gimp thread through four pairs for petal 1. Work in letter order, taking the weaver out round the gimp for pin d, worked as a catch pin. After covering pin f with cloth stitch, take the right-hand gimp thread through the weaver and the centre passive pair. Then work cloth stitch, pin g, cloth stitch and take the gimp thread back to the right through five pairs for petal 2. Work petal 2.

The left-hand gimp thread passes to the left through four pairs for petal 3. In order to keep the gimp thread between the petals a pin should be put in pinhole h, but this must be removed before working hole h. At the bottom pin the gimp is enclosed as at g.

Introduce the new gimp and work the centre ring and tally. Overlap the gimp threads, they will be cut off later.

Select the pairs to begin petal 4 and take the gimp through them to the left.

Work cloth stitch, pin, cloth stitch and continue weaving. Work petal 5.

Begin petal 6 in the same way as petal 4. When complete, the gimp thread is brought round to the right side and laid back across the lace. It will look more attractive if it is threaded between the threads of the pair at z using a sewing needle.

The stem is worked with a single gimp thread. Pairs pass round it as necessary to maintain the curve.

Mounting lace

If lace is to be placed under glass permanently, it is unnecessary to oversew the threads together on the underside of the lace. Use a hook to pull threads through on the six section roundels and tie knots as described on page ooo. In most of the other motifs threads are discarded in the cloth trails which are cut off close to the lace. The threads left at the end are usually tied together to hold them in position. Cut off the bobbins leaving at least 150mm (6 inches) thread. Remove the pins and turn the lace

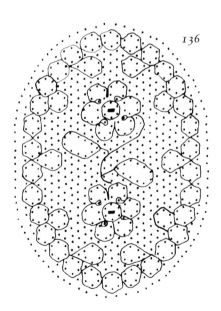

136

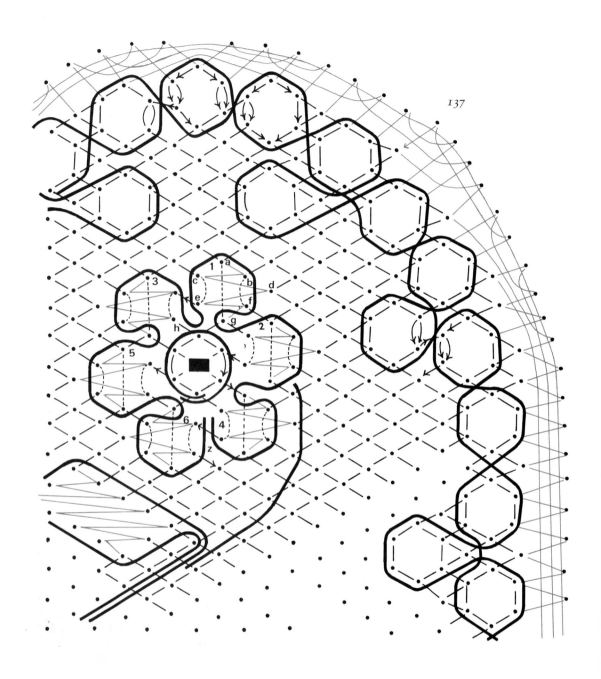

over, the right side is close to the card when the lace is made. Lay the lace on the backing material, this is not yet cut to size. Use a sewing needle to take the threads to the wrong side of the fabric. When the lace is neat and the threads are flat on the back, place it face downwards and lay a piece of iron-on interfacing over the threads. Press firmly with a hot iron, this traps the threads and stiffens the fabric, avoiding frayed edges and making it easier to handle. Cut the fabric to size and mount as required.

Pattern 51. Jabot. Photograph 138.

Any insertion started neatly on a curve or at a point can be used for the centre and any edging selected to be frilled around it; the easily made jabot will enhance a dress shirt or blouse. The lace in the illustration was made using an adaptation of the patterns in photographs 38 and 107A. Photograph 139 shows the laces used and figure 140 gives the prickings. The edging should be started along a horizontal line, refer to diagram 141.

Hang two pairs on pin 1 and twist the threads on either side of the pin three times each to make a firm cord. When required, pairs are hung similarly on 2, 4, 7, 11 and 16. The right-hand pair from 1 and the left-hand pair from 2 work ground pin 3. The right-hand pair from 2 and the left-hand pair from 4 work ground stitch 5, complete the diagonal row with ground stitch 6. Continue to work from 7 to 10, and from 11 to 15. Hang two passive pairs to the left of pin 16. Cover pin 16 with the pairs corded behind the pin.

Ignore the right-hand pair and work the left pair through the passive pairs in cloth stitch. Twist it three times and make a ground stitch with the right-hand pair from 11. Catch pin 17 is placed to the right of both pairs, complete the row to pin 21. It is necessary to introduce the picots immediately; a method is suggested in the diagram. If necessary refer back to diagram 40.

To make the jabot, work the lace required; the length and the fullness are at the discretion of the lacemaker.

Use three pins to indicate half and quarter positions, one passive thread can be pulled to frill the edging. Match the centre pin to the point of the insertion, and the other pins at least 3mm (1 inch) below half way. To achieve a neat join the insertion footside is sewn onto the catch pin stitches on the edging.

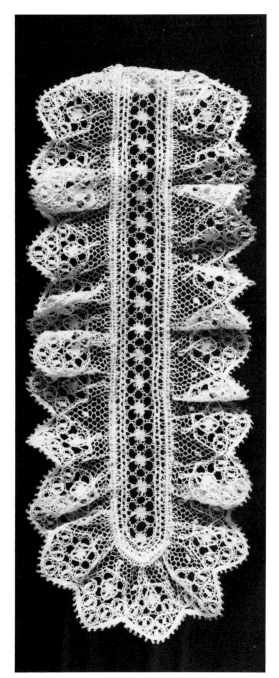

138

115

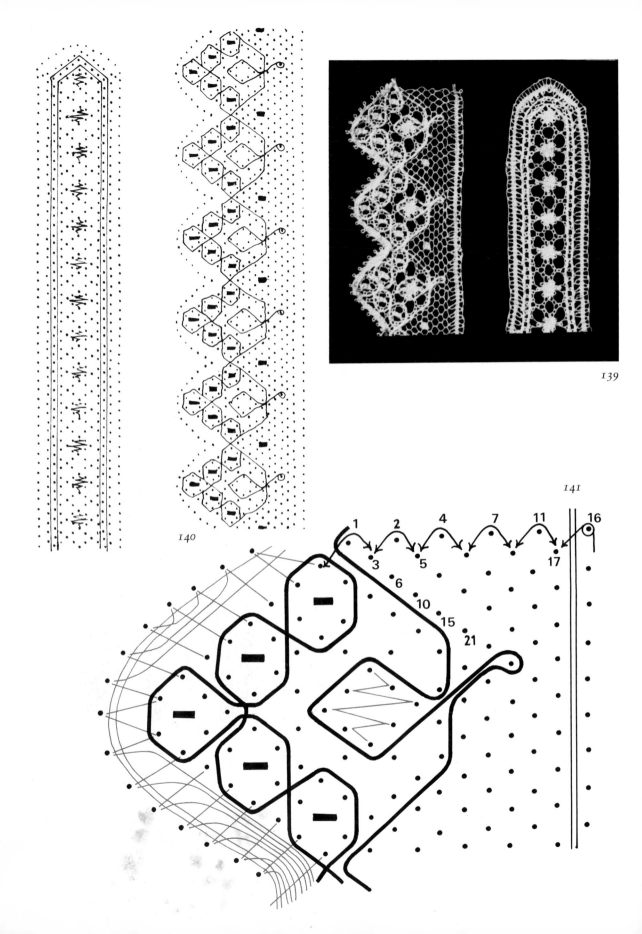

139

140

141

1 2 3 4 5 6 7 10 11 15 16 17 21

Pattern 52. Jabot. Photograph 142.

The final challenge consists of jabot, cuffs and insertion, see also photographs 145 and 147. They all use many of the techniques explained in earlier patterns and are within the scope of anyone who has made and understood the lace in this book. Photograph 143 illustrates the two pieces of lace made independently. A study of photograph 143 and pricking 144 will reveal similarities in starting this and many of the oval or circular motifs. At least two pairs of passives are maintained between gimp and picots, more are acceptable to achieve a neat firm edge. Additional holes may be placed to accommodate honeycomb stitches where pairs cross when travelling to or from picots.

Reference can be made to diagram 104B. Alternatively a cloth stitch and twist is used to cross the pairs. Reference can be made to diagram 106B. As patterns become more complicated there is often more than one way of achieving a desired effect. Strength and appearance are all important and these can be gained through common sense and use of correct technique. A paper copy of the pricking is essential for working out the possible uses of the available pairs. Refer to page 7. To make a strong and neat line across the end the pairs are plaited and discarded as explained on page 68. The two edges should be placed together, gently tucked or slightly gathered and enclosed in a narrow binding.

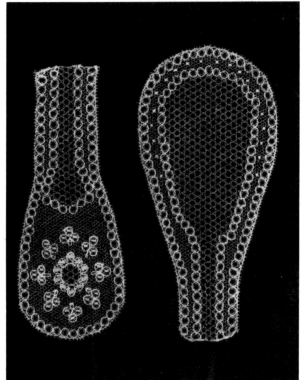

142

143

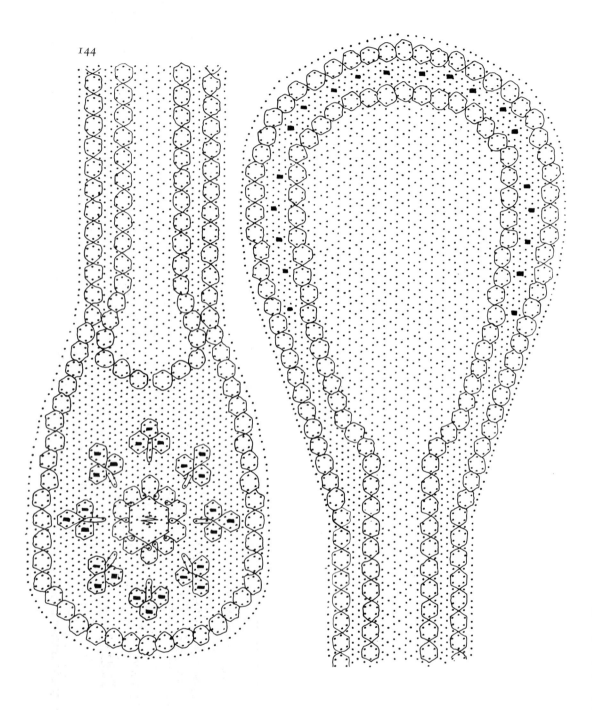

144

Pattern 53. Cuff. Photograph 145.

It has been necessary to print pricking 146 in two
pieces, the actual pricking should be made as one.
One horizontal row of holes is common to both
pieces and used to match the position. All information given for the jabot applies to this pattern. It
can be worked with a footside or picot edge. If it is
to lie upon the cuff fabric the picots will look more
attractive, but a footside edging is more satisfac-
tory if it is to be sewn to the edge of the fabric.

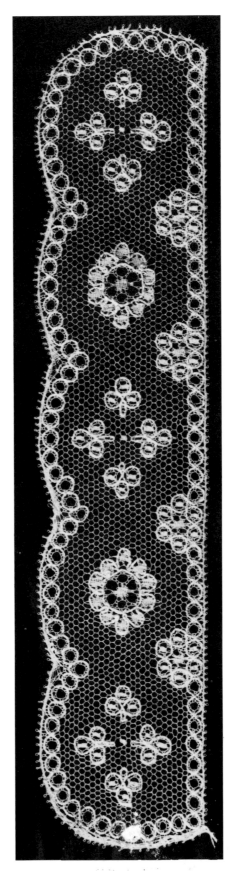

145

119

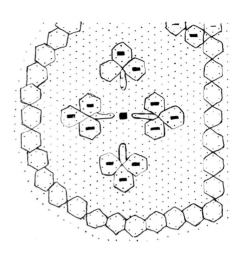

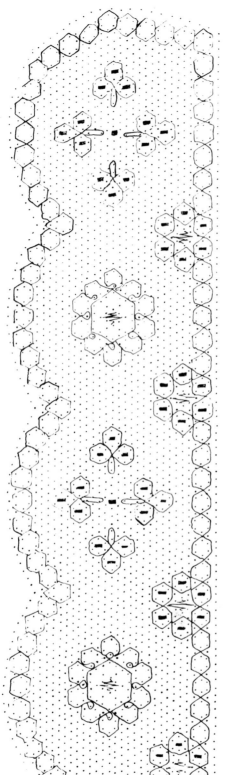

146

Pattern 54. Insertion. Photograph 147.

Worked with a footside edge, this can be used as an insertion on a blouse or skirt. Pricking 148 with the pointed end worked with the footside edge can be used as the centre of a jabot as illustrated on page 115. Instructions for working the footside are given on page 60. With a picot edging it can become an attractive decoration on a small stand-up neckband, or it can be placed over a narrow cuff or across a yoke. Worked from pricking 148 as shown in the photograph, the lace will fit a brush back similar to those on page 98.

147

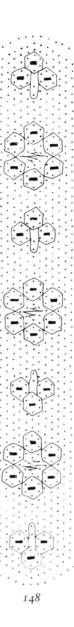

148

Appendix A

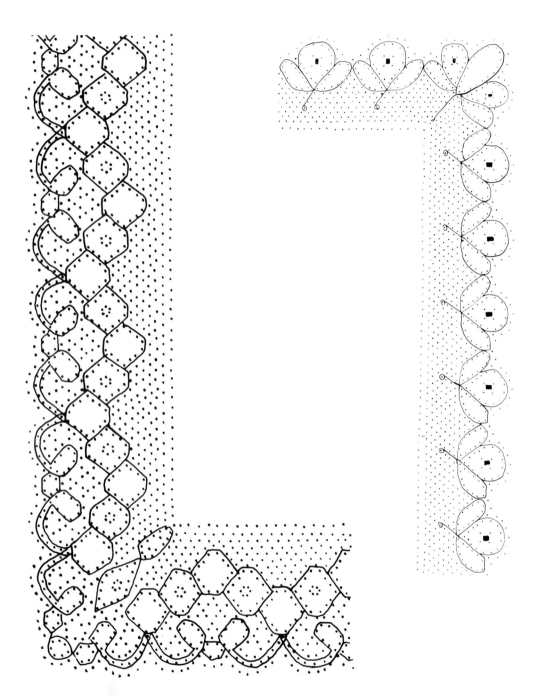

124

Appendix B

Preparation of bobbins and pillow

To wind bobbins

When beginning a pattern, bobbins are used in pairs; knots and thread ends are avoided by putting the thread on bobbins as follows:

(i) Hold the bobbin in the left hand and the thread in the right hand

149

(ii) Wind the thread over and away in a clockwise direction as shown in diagram 149. Wind evenly as much thread as possible onto this bobbin. Cut the thread.

(iii) Take a second bobbin in the left hand and wind half of the thread from the first bobbin onto the second, still in a clockwise direction. This may seem tedious but the thread will tangle and knot if any length is left unwound.

(iv) Refer to diagram 150 and make a hitch on the neck of each bobbin. Allow 150mm (6 inches) of thread between the bobbins.

(v) Temporarily wind the remaining thread round the neck of one of the bobbins, place in a bobbin case or put two or three pairs together with a rubber band.

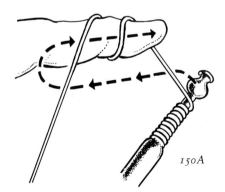

150A

To prepare the pillow

Place the pricking card on the pillow and secure with lace pins at the four corners. Take a hemmed cloth and place it over the lower half of the pillow leaving at least 50mm (2 inches) of pricking visible. Fasten the cloth with one pin at either side.

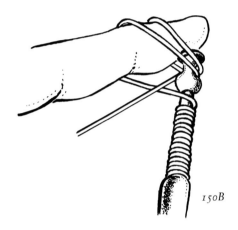

150B

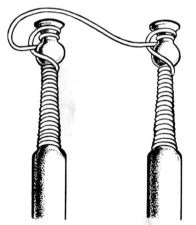

150C

Working information

1. Pins

To put pins into the card, hold the pair of bobbins to the left of the hole in the left hand. Raise the heads of the bobbins to lift the threads and make the hole more easily accessible. A left-handed person should hold the bobbins to the right of the hole and put the pins in with the left hand. Always incline the centre pins back and the side pins outwards. Leave pins in the work for at least 50mm (2 inches), a better tension will result if footside and picot pins are left in position for the length of the pricking.

2. Threads

The distance between pins and bobbins should not exceed 75mm (3 inches). To lengthen a thread hold the bobbin in the right hand across the pillow and turn it towards the lacemaker, loosening the hitch with a pin. This requires practice but is important as thread becomes discoloured when handled.

Knots are never worked into lace. When a knot appears, take another wound bobbin and fasten the thread on a pin behind the work. Lay the new bobbin alongside the bobbin with the knotted thread. Fasten them together with a wire twist or rubber band and work with double thread for at least 25mm (1 inch). Discard the old thread and continue.

3. Re-use of wound bobbins for the new pattern

Take the bobbins and tie together in pairs using reef knots, trim off the ends of thread. Remove the hitches and wind the knot back onto one bobbin, replace the hitches and the bobbins are ready for use. The method for removing knots has been explained above.

4. To move lace on the pillow

This is necessary when making edgings on a flat pillow or lace with a corner.

Cut pieces of felt that are 50mm (2 inches) wide and 25mm, 50mm and 75mm (1, 2 and 3 inches) long. Place them together to give a raised centre and slope at each end, sew together. Place the felt under the pricking so that the pins are embedded in the felt and not the pillow. With care the lace can be moved on the pillow, to effect continuity another piece of pricking is made and placed below the first.

5. To correct errors

The lace has to be undone. As stitches are untwisted, remove pins as necessary. Never remove all the pins at once as the threads cannot be untangled.

Bibliography

Practical information

Channer, C.C. *Lacemaking, Bucks Point Ground.* Dryad Press.

Cook, Bridget M. and Stott, Geraldine. *The Book of Bobbin Lace.* Batsford

Maidment, M. *A Manual of Handmade Bobbin Lace Work.* Batsford.

Nottingham, Pamela. *Bobbin Lace Making.* Batsford.

Nottingham, Pamela. *The Technique of Bobbin Lace.* Batsford.

Nottingham, Pamela. *The Technique of Bucks Point Lace.* Batsford.

Stott, Geraldine and Cook, Bridget M. *100 Traditional Bobbin Lace Patterns.* Batsford.

Stott, Geraldine. *Visual Introduction to Bucks Point Lace.* Batsford.

Stott, Geraldine. *The Bobbin Lace Manual.* Batsford.

Sutton, Edna and Moseley, M. *Bees, Birds and Butterflies in Lace.* Batsford.

Historical information

Bullock, A.M., *Lace and Lacemaking*, Batsford 1981.

Freeman, Charles, *Pillow Lace in the East Midlands*, Luton Museum and Art Gallery 1958.

Wright, Thomas, *The Romance of the Lace Pillow*, Minet 1971.

Index